For Joseph and Denise Rodolphe

THE CRUSADER KING

THE CRUSADER KING

RICHARD THE LIONHEARTED

c.73-27

BY

RICHARD SUSKIND

ILLUSTRATED BY WILLIAM SAUTS BOCK

LITTLE, BROWN AND COMPANY

BOSTON   TORONTO

FIRST EDITION

T 04/73

Library of Congress Cataloging in Publication Data

Suskind, Richard.
  The crusader king, Richard the Lionhearted.

  SUMMARY: A biography of the second king of the
Plantagenet dynasty who lived in England only six months
during his ten year reign.
  Bibliography: p.
  1. Richard I, King of England, 1157-1199--Juvenile
literature. [1. Richard I, King of England, 1157-1199.
2. Great Britain--History--Richard I, 1189-1199]
I. Bock, William Sauts, 1939-   illus. II. Title.
DA207.S87   942.03'2'0924 [B] [92]   72-6728
ISBN 0-316-82250-7

Published simultaneously in Canada
by Little, Brown & Company (Canada) Limited

PRINTED IN THE UNITED STATES OF AMERICA

CONTENTS

THE CRUSADER KING

THE YOUNG DUKE

1

KING HENRY learned the good news on the morning of September 8, 1157, as he was returning to Oxford after a successful campaign against the Scots. He was still several miles from the castle, riding at the head of his troops, when a messenger galloped up and told him that his wife, Eleanor, had just given birth to a boy. Henry was delighted. "The king did shout with joy," wrote his secretary, Peter of Blois, "and reward the bearer of these happy tidings with a piece of gold. Then he dismounted and kneeled on the grassy verge of the road and gave thanks to God."

Henry II, the founder of the Plantagenet dynasty, had reason to be pleased. Although he was the most powerful monarch in Christendom, the ruler of England, Ireland, and nearly all of western France, he badly needed sons both to carry on his name and to help him govern his domain during his lifetime.

These domains were divided into huge fiefs, or estates, each ruled by a powerful baron who was Henry's "man"—that is, one who had sworn oaths of homage and fealty to the king, agreeing to supply him with a fixed number of knights and sergeants every year for a "quarantine"—forty days—of service in the royal army, and to support him in all his conflicts. The oaths of homage and fealty were the cornerstones of feudalism, the system which had held sway in Europe since the time of Charlemagne, four centuries earlier.

Many of Henry's barons, however, bitterly resented their inferior position. They were proud, arrogant men who considered themselves the equal of any ruler. Did they not hold the power of life and death over the lesser nobles to whom they in turn had given fiefs, as well as over the thousands of serfs and villeins who farmed their lands? So they often plotted against the king, or openly defied him, and it was only by traveling constantly from one part of his domains to another that Henry was able to keep them in check, to collect taxes, and to administer the king's justice.

This was a wearisome business, even for a man of Henry's boundless energy. By placing sons in charge of the various counties and duchies, the king hoped to lift some of the burden of rule from his own shoulders. His and Eleanor's firstborn son had died in infancy. Their second, two-year-old

Henry, would help him govern—and was slated to inherit—England, Normandy, and Anjou. This new arrival, the king decided, would be given Aquitaine, Eleanor's duchy in southwest France.

And so, within hours after he had first drawn breath, Richard Plantagenet became Duke of Aquitaine.

Many years passed before Richard took charge of his domains. He was put in the care of a foster mother until he was weaned and then turned over to a succession of tutors and guardians. He spent his childhood mostly in Normandy, moving from castle to castle with his parents, his older brother Henry, his younger brothers Geoffrey and John, and his three sisters.

It was not a happy household. His parents quarreled constantly, partly because they were both strong-willed people accustomed to having their own way, but mostly because King Henry, eleven years younger than Eleanor, was repeatedly unfaithful to her and had several children by other women. Moreover, the king further insulted Eleanor by bringing up these illegitimate children as part of the royal household—"so that the queen's eyes were daily offended by the evidence of the king's base passions."

Richard sided with his mother in these quarrels and grew up with deep feelings of resentment toward his father. Nevertheless, he learned many valuable lessons from watching Henry rule. He saw, for instance, how the king rewarded his friends and loyal advisers by giving them lands and titles and rich heiresses to marry, and how he punished his enemies with utter ruthlessness. An example of the latter occurred in 1164, when the Celtic chieftains of Wales erupted over the border into England and ravaged the countryside with fire and sword. These chieftains had earlier given sons and daughters to Henry as hostages for their good behavior. Henry now blinded the boys, cut the noses and ears off the girls, and sent the mutilated hostages back to their parents. No one seemed to think his action unusually cruel. In harsh times like the Middle Ages it was natural to behave harshly. Richard himself, as we shall see, was capable of far crueler actions.

Richard also witnessed the quarrel between King Henry and his best friend, Thomas à Becket. The quarrel began when Thomas, with the king's help, was appointed Archbishop of Canterbury. This was the most important religious office in the kingdom and, through Thomas, Henry hoped to gain control of the Church's affairs in England. Things did not work out that way, however, for Thomas, a devout Christian, thereafter put duty before friendship and sided with the pope rather than the king in the struggle between Church and State. Matters grew steadily worse between the two men until one day Henry, in a fit of rage, exclaimed, "Oh, would that he were dead!" A group of Henry's knights overheard him, took matters into their own hands, and murdered Thomas in Canterbury Cathedral—perhaps the most famous murder in English history.

Although the king had not ordered the murder, his angry words had been responsible for it. He atoned by putting on penitent's robes and walking barefoot into Canterbury so that the awed inhabitants could trace his bloody footprints down the cobbled streets. When he reached the cathedral, he fell to his knees before the tomb of Saint Thomas and allowed himself to be scourged with whips like a common criminal.

In 1167, when Richard was ten years old, Henry and Eleanor separated. The king continued to spend most of his time in England and Normandy, and soon began to live openly with Rosamund Clifford, a beautiful noblewoman known in popular ballads as "Fair Rosamund." Eleanor, bitter and resentful, retired to her castle in Poitiers, the capital of Aquitaine, accompanied by several of the children. It was there that Richard grew to manhood and completed his training as a knight.

This training had begun three years earlier, in Normandy, when a priest had taught Richard to read and write French and a smattering of Latin, and to do simple sums. Richard had also learned to hold courtly conversation with the ladies, to dance, and to appreciate music and poetry. He liked poetry so much, in fact, that in later years he even wrote a few verses which were sung by wandering troubadours in castles throughout England and France.

By far the most important part of a knight's training, however, was in the arts of war, and now, in Poitiers, Richard began work in earnest. Under the watchful eye of a master of arms, he spent hours every day on the martial practice grounds outside the walls of the castle. He built up his strength and endurance by running round and round the field wearing a full suit of chain mail, which weighed from forty to sixty pounds. He practiced wielding the sword, the mace, the two-handed Danish battle-ax, and the scramasax, or dagger. Using blunt weapons, he fought mock battles with the other noble youths, and gave—and received—many hard knocks. He learned to bear heat and cold without complaint, to go without food or water for long periods of time, to stay awake when he could hardly keep his eyes open. And he spent at least two hours a day in the most knightly of all exercises, "tilting at the quintain."

The quintain was a T-shaped construction of wood about ten feet high, with the crossbar of the T on a pivot so that it would swing freely. Suspended from one end of the crossbar was the carved wooden figure of a Saracen dressed in a battered old suit of armor. From the other end of the crossbar hung a sack of earth that served as a counterweight. Richard and the other knights-in-training would mount their destriers, or war horses, line up about twenty-five yards from the quintain, and charge it one after the other. As he charged, each youth would couch his lance so that the hilt nestled snugly against his right side and the steel point jutted out beyond the left of his mount's head. At the last moment he would stick his legs straight out before him, bracing his feet against the stirrups and his back against the high cantle of the saddle, duck down behind the kite-shaped shield that hung from his left arm, and give his battle cry. If his destrier charged straight and true, the point of the lance would ram into the figure of the Saracen and send it whirling in a circle, followed by the counterweight. If the horse flinched or pulled up too soon, however, the sack of earth would slam into the youth's back and sometimes tumble him out of the saddle. You can imagine his embarrassment and the shouts of laughter from the others when this happened.

Richard soon demonstrated that extraordinary talent for fighting which was to cover him with glory in later years. "Few squires were willing to break lances with him," wrote the chronicler, Richard of Devizes, "and he sought out grizzled veterans to test his mettle." This is not surprising, for by the age of fourteen Richard was more than six feet tall, as strong and broad-shouldered as most men. He was handsome, too, with blue eyes, a girl's complexion, and flaming red-gold hair which fell nearly to his shoulders. He had not yet acquired the nickname *Coeur de Lion*—Lionhearted—but was known as "Richard Yea-and-Nay" because of his bluntness and stubbornness. He spoke out boldly at all times, and if he said yea or nay to a proposal, no amount of pleading or arguing could make him change his mind. Indeed, it was dangerous to plead or argue too vehemently with Richard. Like his father, he had the ungovernable Plantagenet temper and was capable of falling into a black fury during which he sometimes committed acts that he later regretted.

When he was not training with his weapons or actually at war, Richard was usually out hunting. Early in the morning the chief huntsman would sound a clarion call on his horn, cry "Up, seigneurs, we go to the forest!" and Richard and his companions, mounted on fleet palfreys and carrying hunting lances, would follow the pack of baying hounds into the nearby forest. Hunting—"the mystery of the woods"—was more than just a sport in the Middle Ages. It was a principal source of meat, since the domestic animals—sheep, cattle, pigs —were mostly scrawny creatures whose flesh was only suitable to be salted down in barrels.

Much of Europe was still covered with forests in which deer, boar, rabbits, wolves, and other animals abounded. The forests were reserved for the nobles, however, and if a peasant was caught poaching in them, he was severely punished. If he merely chased a deer and "made it paunt," he was fined as much as a year's income. And if he actually killed the animal, he often had his right hand cut off and was told to "wear the wolf's head"—that is, to go into exile and join one of the bands of outlaws, most of them crippled, that were driven from village to village and usually died of starvation or exposure in the first severe winter. King Henry was especially hard on poachers, hanging some and castrating others. He also forbade any peasant who lived near a forest to keep a dog unless it was "lawed" by having three toes cut off one of its front paws so that it could not hunt.

The most dangerous game in the forest was wild boar. The chronicler Gervase of Bonville has left us an exciting anecdote of a hunt in which Richard and his companions trapped one of these great beasts in a dense mass of underbrush. "Duke Richard and the others dismounted, took up their lances, and placed themselves on all sides of the thicket," wrote Gervase. "From its center there rose grunts and squeals of rage, and yelps of anguish from the dogs, and then there came a rattling of branches and the beast appeared, red of eye and with slaver dripping from its jaws. It charged at once and my lord Vulgrin of Angoulême was bowled off his feet and slashed on both legs by the gleaming tushes. Duke Richard, bellowing like a boar himself, came running and plunged his lance again and again into the beast. His boon companions did likewise, and soon its heart was pierced and it gave up the ghost."

After the game had been killed, it was butchered on the spot. The lungs and intestines were thrown to the dogs, then the carcass was trussed to a branch and carried back to the castle. When the hunters returned, often after spending from sunrise to sunset at the chase, they washed the blood and dirt from their hands and relaxed before the fire while the cooks prepared the food.

At that time people ate only two meals a day, breakfast and supper. A popular jingle of the twelfth century ran:

> Rise at five, dine at nine,
> Sup at five, to bed at nine,
> Is how we live to be ninety and nine.

All this outdoor activity gave the men huge appetites; by our standards, Richard's average workday supper was an enormous feast. Platter after platter of meat appeared on the table, followed by bowls of fruit and nuts, all washed down with quantities of wine, cider, and a fermented pear juice called perry. The nobles ate a white bread known as Our Lord's bread because the figure of Christ was imprinted on each loaf. The sergeants and others who sat "below the salt" ate a coarse brown bread called wastel. The meat was usually eaten on a trencher (wooden plate) or large slice of stale bread, which soaked up the gravy and was given to the poor afterward. If a man was a hearty eater, as Richard was, he was called a good trencherman—an expression we still use today. At the end of the meal, pages would pass around bowls of water so that the nobles could wash their hands.

Another of Richard's favorite peace-time activities was jousting at tournaments. Although the Church forbade these "war-games" and refused Christian burial to men who were killed in them, they remained tremendously popular. They were not the formal affairs of later centuries, in which strictly regulated single combats took place, but brutal free-for-alls, called melees, in which many knights jousted with each other until they were either unhorsed or became exhausted and left the field. The victor in each encounter had the right to hold the defeated knight's horse and armor for ransom. A few "knights errant" earned handsome if precarious livings by following what might be called the tournament trail. Besides the money he earned by winning his jousts, the knight who demonstrated the most valor and endurance at a tournament was awarded a prize by the "Queen of Love and Beauty," a young noblewoman chosen for this task. The prize could be a gold chaplet set with precious stones, or a fine helmet, or sometimes a sword or other piece of equipment.

All of Henry's sons loved tournaments. Prince Henry, for

example, used to travel halfway across England with his tutor in chivalry, William Marshal, to take part in one. Although he was a poor horseman, clumsy with his weapons and not very strong, Henry never lost a joust. Not daring to offend their heir to the throne, his opponents unhorsed themselves at the first touch of his lance! Besides, if a knight was rash enough to unhorse the prince, he would then have to joust with that "invincible lance" William Marshal, probably the finest knight errant in the kingdom. Geoffrey, too, took part in many tournaments—indeed, as we shall see, in one too many for his own good. We have no record of the number of times Richard participated in these affairs, but we may be sure that he was strong and fierce enough to hold his own, even against older and more experienced warriors.

Still another sort of diversion was provided by troubadours and minstrels who wandered here and there about the continent. Many of these medieval entertainers came to Eleanor's court in Poitiers, where they knew they would be given food and lodging for as long as they chose to stay, and sent on their way again with a wallet full of bread and meat and a few coins to clink together. Especially welcome were troubadours returned from Outremer (French for "Beyond-the-sea"), as the kingdom of Jerusalem was known, for they sang of the glories of the First Crusade—of Godfrey of Bouillon, "the Perfect Christian Knight," who had captured the Holy City in 1099; of Bohemond of Taranto, who by guile and valor had made himself Prince of Antioch; of King Baldwin I, Godfrey's younger brother, and his famous Arabian stallion, Gazelle; of the fighting religious orders, the Knights Templar and the Knights Hospitaller.

Richard and the other noble lords and ladies sat on wooden benches at the round table in the great hall of the castle, while the troubadours sang their *chansons de geste*, accompanying themselves on the lute and the viol. If it was winter, a log or two would be burning in the fireplace and the air would be thick with smoke from the oil lamps placed here and there (for candles were too expensive except for the most special occasions). Oriental tapestries and rugs, brought back from the East by returning Crusaders, would hang from the thick stone walls and help keep out the icy drafts that came through the window slits; and straw and sheepskins would be heaped about the floor so that the squires and pages and sergeants could recline in comfort.

Queen Eleanor was perhaps less entranced than the rest of the audience by these tales of blood and glory. As a dark-eyed beauty of twenty-five she had accompanied her first husband, King Louis VII of France, on the Second Crusade (1147–1149). She thus knew at first hand of the difficulties of life in Outremer—of the heat and dust, the flies, the constant threat of Saracen attack, the strange diseases that could kill

a healthy man in a matter of days. But Richard's imagination was undoubtedly stimulated by the *chansons de geste*. They made him eager to go on a crusade himself, to travel over the sea and do battle with the infidel for the glory of God. First, however, he had to gain a prize closer to home: the throne of England.

Shortly after his fourteenth birthday, Richard underwent two important ceremonies: he was formally invested as Duke of Aquitaine, and thus, with his mother, became joint ruler of the duchy; and he was knighted. The latter ceremony, the more important of the two (one was born a duke, but knighthood had to be earned), took place in the Church of Saint Hilary in Poitiers and was attended by King Henry and several of his leading nobles.

Richard spent the night before the ceremony in the chapel, kneeling in a "vigil of arms" before the altar on which his weapons were laid, praying to God to make him worthy of the honor he was about to receive. At dawn he went back to the castle, bathed, and dressed in spotless garments. First he put on a robe of white silk, symbolic of chastity. Over this he placed a scarlet cloak, symbolic of the blood he must be ready to spill in defense of the Church. He wore brown boots to remind him that man is mortal and must return to the earth, and a white belt which signified virginity. A round spot, the size of a monk's tonsure, was shaved in the center of his crown, for it was considered a mark of devotion to God to give up one's hair.

When these preparations were completed, he was escorted to the chapel again, where he heard a solemn mass and then was asked the ritual questions by the bishop: "Why do you wish to become a knight? Is it with the hope of gaining treasure? Is it that men may show you honor?"

To these questions Richard made the ritual replies: "No. It is that I may serve Christ the Lord with a pure mind and heart. It is that I may devote the strength of my arm to the defense of His Holy Church. It is that I may aid those in distress, protect the weak against the strong and the poor against the rich, and maintain my knightly honor and integrity at all times and in all places."

Then King Henry stepped forward. He was now forty years old, a stocky, pot-bellied but still powerful man, with a red face and bulging, bloodshot eyes. He picked up Richard's sword, with its gold-and-jewel encrusted hilt, from the altar and gave him the "accolade" by tapping him with the flat of the blade three times on the right shoulder. "In the name of Christ, Saint George, and Saint Denis," he said, "I dub thee knight. Be gallant, be courteous, be loyal."

Everyone then left the chapel and Richard's brothers and sisters handed him the rest of his equipment. After he had put on his armor, hung his sword at his waist, and strapped his golden spurs to his heels, he gave a demonstration of his horsemanship. Without touching the stirrups, he leaped into the saddle on his destrier and galloped round and round the assembly, while everyone cheered and applauded. Then he showed "largesse" by distributing gifts to the Church, to the peasants and beggars who had gathered to watch the festivities, and to the minstrels and troubadours who had come to entertain the guests. The ceremony was now officially over and everyone trooped into the castle, where tables were loaded with food and drink, and spent the rest of the day feasting and celebrating.

Sir Richard Plantagenet, Duke of Aquitaine, was ready to assume the responsibilities of manhood.

THE DEVIL'S BROOD

2

IN THE SUMMER of 1173, when Richard was sixteen, Aquitaine was invaded by an army of English and Norman knights led by King Henry himself. The sights and smells of war were seen everywhere, for the king was in a towering rage and had ordered his men to "harry" the land—that is, to loot, kill, and destroy as much as possible.

In all medieval warfare there was nothing worse than a harrying. Cottages, barns, and fields of ripening grain burned and smoldered, sending columns of black greasy smoke into the air. Dead horses and cows littered the landscape, the legs sticking up out of their swollen bodies like pins out of a pincushion. Villeins and serfs of both sexes and all ages—those who had been too slow in running to their lord's castle when the churchbells clanged the alarm—lay about here and there, some with their throats slit, others hacked to death by swords, pierced by lances, or with arrows jutting out of their bodies. Many of the younger women were sprawled in the obscene postures in which their violators and murderers had left them. Chivalry existed in the Middle Ages, but only between members of the nobility. Peasants were considered little better than animals.

The war had begun the previous spring, when Richard and his brothers Henry and Geoffrey had raised the standard of revolt against their father. Prince Henry had rebelled because, although he was a married man of eighteen and had been crowned joint ruler of the kingdom, his father treated him like a child and gave him no authority. Geoffrey had rebelled simply because he was a born intriguer and loved betrayal for its own sake. Richard needed no excuse to rebel, but had one in the fact that his father would not give him permission to marry King Louis of France's youngest daughter, Alice, to whom he had been betrothed since childhood. (This was just a pretext, however, for Richard was really interested in marrying Berengaria, the daughter of King Sancho VI of Navarre, whose domains bordered on Aquitaine.)

The real instigator of the "Great Rebellion," however, had been Queen Eleanor. She took revenge on her unfaithful husband by turning his sons against him. She actively encouraged them to rebel and even arranged for them to be helped by King Louis, her former husband.

King Henry's numerous other enemies hastened to take

advantage of the situation. The barons of Yorkshire and Norfolk rose up in arms, and King William of Scotland led his
kilted clansmen into the border shires of Northumberland and
Cumberland. "The king was sore beset," wrote Roger of
Hoveden, a member of the court, "and called down God's
curse upon his sins. In his rage and despair he said that his
bastards were his true sons, for they had remained loyal,
while his true sons were the bastards."

But Henry was not a man to despair for long. He swiftly
gathered an army of loyal English and Norman knights and
set out to quell the revolt. First he defeated and captured
King William, releasing him only after William had paid a
ransom of ten thousand pounds and signed a humiliating
treaty. Then he crushed the rebels in Yorkshire and Norfolk,
confiscating part of their lands and sending their leaders into
exile. With these two threats eliminated, he crossed the
Channel to deal with his wife and sons.

The king had a stroke of luck at the start of his campaign,
for his knights captured Eleanor as she was attempting to
make her way, disguised as a man, to the court of King
Louis in Paris. She was sent under guard to Winchester castle
in England and confined there for the next sixteen years.
Prince Henry, the handsome but empty-headed heir to the
throne, surrendered soon afterward. Without Eleanor to support and advise him, he could not stand against his father.

He too was sent to England, although he was allowed to keep his freedom. Clever, sly, fifteen-year-old Geoffrey was next to give up. He saw that the rebellion had no chance of success and he was anxious to return to Brittany, where he had recently married the heiress to the duchy and thus had become Duke of Brittany.

Only Richard, the most stubborn and warlike of Henry's sons, fought on. He continued the unequal contest until the winter of 1174, by which time the peasants of Aquitaine were threatened with famine. Then, seeing the hopelessness of further resistance, he threw himself at his father's feet and begged his forgiveness. It was an emotional scene. "The tears coursed freely down their cheeks," wrote an anonymous chronicler. "Then King Henry raised Richard to his feet, gave him the kiss of peace, and bade him return to Poitiers and restore order to the duchy."

This proved to be a long and troublesome business, for many of the Aquitainian nobles, enraged at their queen's imprisonment, openly defied Henry and Richard. It was during this period, which lasted nearly ten years, that Richard became a master tactician as well as a renowned fighter. He studied the art of siege warfare until, it was said, he could spot the weakness in any fortress ever built. He learned how to mine, or tunnel, beneath the wall of a castle so that it would collapse in a heap of rubble; how to use scaling ladders, battering rams, and a variety of catapults. His army was composed mostly of mercenary Flemings—hard-bitten professional soldiers from the Low Countries, many of them thieves, murderers, and runaway serfs. These "froth and scum of chivalry" worshipped Richard, for he was as quick to reward success as he was to punish failure, and he was the equal of any of them in hand-to-hand combat. At their head, he subdued castle after castle and extended his rule through Gascony to the foothills of the Pyrenees mountains. A splendid example of his tactical skill at this time was the siege of Taillebourg, which he undertook when he was twenty-one.

Taillebourg was one of the most heavily fortified castles in Aquitaine. It was surrounded by triple walls and a triple ditch, contained a year's supply of food, ample water, and was garrisoned by a thousand men under the command of Geoffrey of Rancogne, an experienced warrior. Although the castle had no obvious weaknesses, Richard was unwilling to settle down to a long siege, so he resolved on a stratagem. First, he burned the nearby villages and farms, killing the livestock and destroying the shooks of recently harvested grain. Then, toward evening, he pitched his tents just beyond bowshot of the castle's walls and told his men to laugh and shout and stagger around as if they were taking part in a drunken revel.

Geoffrey responded as Richard had hoped he would. In-

furiated at Richard's "insolence," he opened the gates to Taillebourg and led the garrison in a furious sally on the camp.
But the Flemings were ready and waiting. They repulsed the
attack, then chased Geoffrey back through the open gates and
captured the castle.

This constant campaigning, however, at an age when
modern youths are still in school, took its toll of Richard's
health. He came down with a type of malaria known as quar-
tan ague, and was troubled by it for the rest of his life. Re-
current attacks of the fever made him shiver as though his
bones would break. Oddly enough, the ague was responsible
for Richard's nickname, Lionhearted. The contemporary historian Gerald of Wales said that God had given him the
disease "to repress the over-fierce workings of his mind. But
he, like the lion—yea, more than the lion—that he was,
seemed rather to be influenced by the ague as by a goad; for
while thus continually trembling, he remained intrepid in his
determination to make the whole world tremble at him."
Gerald's description became widely known and soon people
everywhere began to call Richard the Lionhearted.

Richard's reconquest of Aquitaine was interrupted in 1176
by a brief war with Count Raymond of Toulouse, his powerful neighbor to the southeast. Private wars of this sort were
strictly forbidden by the pope. They violated the "Truce of

God," which forbade Christian fighting Christian from Wednesday evening after vespers until the following Monday morning of every week. A man who violated the Truce of God, read the papal proclamation, was to be "banished and driven out of his country, and shall make his way into exile at Jerusalem." The punishment thus served two purposes: it helped keep the peace in Europe, and it insured a steady supply of men to fight the Saracen in the Holy Land.

Despite the Truce of God, however, private wars erupted constantly. They often started over trifles—an imagined insult, a disputed boundary—and went on for generation after generation, until the original cause of the war had been forgotten. The object of the war was usually not to kill the enemy but to take him prisoner and hold him for ransom. If the captured noble was unable to pay the ransom immediately, he was imprisoned in the dungeons beneath his captor's castle until he could raise the money, which sometimes took months or even years. These dungeons were known as *oubliettes*, which is French for "forgotten places," and were simply holes in the ground with a trap door in the ceiling. Men confined for long periods in these dank, lightless pits often went blind.

Richard's private war against Count Raymond was based on firmer ground than were most such affairs. The count owed allegiance to the Duke of Aquitaine but had refused to recognize Richard as his overlord. In effect he had said: "What!

Count Raymond of Toulouse, one of the most powerful nobles in Christendom, recognize a stripling as his overlord! Never!"

Richard soon proved himself no ordinary stripling, however, but a commander of genius. While Raymond was still leisurely gathering his forces, Richard stormed across the border, penned the nobles up in their castles, and burned and slaughtered in the surrounding countryside until the count, appalled at the demon he had let loose, begged for mercy. The surrender took place in a field outside of Toulouse. Raymond and Richard met in the center of a circle formed by their armed retainers. Raymond kneeled and placed his hands between Richard's and swore the oath of homage and fealty. Henceforth, he agreed, he would hold his country as a fief from Richard and would fulfill his customary feudal obligations. This was a bitter pill for Raymond to swallow and he rebelled on several occasions thereafter. Richard put down the rebellions with ease, and at last, by marrying Raymond to one of his sisters, he made a firm ally of him.

Richard's growing prestige aroused the envy of his brothers, however, and in 1183 Prince Henry, supported by that inveterate troublemaker Geoffrey, demanded that Richard recognize him as overlord of Aquitaine. Richard refused in his usual blunt manner, and immediately afterward Henry and Geoffrey invaded Aquitaine with an army of mercenaries.

It was at this time that people began to call the Plantaganet family "the Devil's brood," for a rumor went around that they

were descended from Mélusine, the wife of a mythical crea-
ture. The rumor was widely accepted as true by the illiterate
and superstitious populace, for why else, they asked one another, would blood brothers ravage each other's lands and
slaughter each other's villeins and serfs? Richard himself may
have believed the story, for when a high official of the Church
rebuked him for fighting his brothers, he said: "Do not de-
prive us of our heritage. We cannot help acting like devils."

The war ended abruptly when Prince Henry came down
with dysentery and died—whether of the disease or the medi-
cal treatment, we cannot be sure. The science of medicine in
those days, particularly in Europe, was so primitive that a sick
or wounded man was at least as likely to be killed as cured by
his physician. Bleeding, for example, was a favorite practice.
Whether the sick man had a headache, a cold, or some truly
dreadful disease such as cholera, a vein would be opened in
his arm and as much as a pint of blood removed. If this treatment was repeated often enough at close intervals, as it sometimes was, the patient died simply of loss of blood. Wounds
were treated with equal crudity. Amputations, for instance,
were performed with an ax, while five or six men held the
screaming patient on a table. The stump of the amputated
limb was then plunged into a vat of boiling pitch. This
stopped the bleeding but the pain was so excruciating that
most patients died of shock.

With Prince Henry dead, Richard was next in line for the

throne—but only if his father formally recognized him as heir. The king summoned his sons to Normandy to discuss the matter. He would name Richard his heir, he said, if Richard would turn Aquitaine over to his younger brother John (who was known as "Lackland" because he had no domains of his own). Richard asked for a few days to think it over, but that same evening he rode south to Poitier's, leaving behind an angry message in which he said he would not give up his beloved duchy to anyone for any reason.

King Henry flew into a rage when he read the message. Turning to John, who was just sixteen, he said: "You're old enough to claim your inheritance. Take it!"

Within a week the tormented peasants of Aquitaine—the real victims of these family squabbles—were once again suffering at the hands of the "unnatural Plantagenets," for John and Geoffrey (the latter was always ready for a bit of mischief) invaded the duchy with hired troops. Richard struck back vigorously, routed the invaders in battle, and sent his brothers "flying discomfited" over the border into Brittany. At this point King Henry, regretting his angry words, summoned his unruly sons to England and patched up peace between them.

Though it was an uneasy peace, always threatening to break down, it gave Richard a much-needed breathing space. He used the time to cultivate an alliance and friendship with the new ruler of France, Philip Augustus, who had taken over when his father, King Louis, died in 1180.

It was an odd sort of friendship, for it would be hard to find two men less alike than Richard and Philip. Where Richard was blunt and forthright, Philip, eight years younger, was subtle and devious. Where Richard was big and strong, Philip was small and slight—and blind in one eye to boot. Where Richard was rather dour and stern, Philip was known for his wit and humor. On one occasion, for example, Philip was ordered by his physician to mix his wine with water. "May I drink them in separate goblets?" Philip asked. The physician pondered for a moment, then agreed. At dinner that evening, Philip drank a large goblet of wine but rejected the goblet of water which his servant then placed before him. "I'm no longer thirsty," he said, with a sly glance at his physician. Philip was also a much better administrator than Richard. During his reign (1180–1223) the main streets of Paris were paved, the construction of the famous cathedral of Notre Dame was begun, the first Louvre was built, and France itself became one of the chief powers in Europe.

But while things went well between Richard and Philip, they went very badly between Richard and his father. There was now a barely concealed hatred between them. It became increasingly obvious that Henry had no intention of naming Richard his heir but would divide his lands so that one of his other sons would receive the crown. Geoffrey was eliminated from the running in 1186, when he was trampled to death by his destrier after being unhorsed at a tournament. However, this still left the king's favorite, John, a handsome but treacherous young man who was to cause Richard endless trouble. To strengthen John's claim to the throne, Henry tried to marry him to Philip Augustus's sister Alice, although she was still theoretically engaged to Richard (and although it was widely believed that Alice, who had been living at the English court for many years, had become the lustful old king's mistress).

Richard was well aware of his father's scheming. He grew more and more angry and bitter, and at last, determined to have what was rightfully his, he gathered his forces and prepared to strike.

Meanwhile, nearly two thousand miles away in Outremer, events were taking place that were to play a crucial role in Richard's subsequent career. Indeed, they were to give him lasting fame as the "Crusader King."

While Richard had been engaged in destructive family quarrels in Europe, a new figure had risen to power in the Moslem world. His name was Saladin and he was the sultan of Egypt, Syria, and Iraq.

Saladin regarded the Christian kingdom of Jerusalem as a "thorn in Islam's flesh" and was determined to pluck it out.

In the summer of 1187, at the head of about twenty thousand
Moslem warriors, he crossed the Jordan River and began his
campaign by besieging the Christian castle in Tiberias.

Guy of Lusignan, the king of Jerusalem, was a day's march
away, in Sephoria, trying to decide upon a course of action.
His more realistic advisers said he should let Tiberias fall, that
it was an unimportant fortress and that the Moslems would
only loot it and then return across the Jordan. But others, particularly the Grand Master of the Knights Templar, said this
would be shameful and unchivalrous behavior and that the
king was obliged to muster his army and march to the attack.
Guy, a weak and impulsive ruler, took the Grand Master's
advice, and on the morning of July 3, 1187, the Christian
army, also numbering about twenty thousand men, set out
over the rocky hills of Galilee.

There was not a drop of water to be had between Sephoria
and Lake Tiberias. Late in the afternoon, weary and thirsty,
the Christians reached the Horns of Hattin, a pair of hills
which rose above the plain near the lake. They were unable to
get water, however, because Saladin's army was installed on
the plain, so they made camp on one of the hills.

The Christians spent a miserable night. Not only were they
tortured by thirst, but the Moslems set fire to the dry shrubs
covering the sides of the hill and a thick cloud of acrid smoke
settled over the camp. Under cover of the darkness and

smoke, Saladin's troops moved up to the base of the hill until, as one Arab historian wrote, "not a cat could slip through the net."

The Moslems attacked with the dawn. They were fresh and confident, inspired by the leadership of the great sultan. The Christian foot soldiers had room for only one thought in their heads—water. They surged in an undisciplined mass down the hill toward the lake gleaming tantalizingly in the distance, and were cut to pieces by the Saracens. Christian honor was saved only by the knights who, their swollen tongues protruding from their mouths, turned back charge after charge of the Moslem cavalry.

By noon the Christians were exhausted. They moved King Guy's red tent to the top of the hill, gathered around it, and prepared for a last-ditch defense. Saladin's young son, al-Afdal, witnessing his first battle, described the last moments of the debacle as follows:

"When the Christian King had withdrawn to the top of the hill, his knights made a gallant charge and drove the Moslems back upon my father. I watched with dismay. He turned pale, then red, pulled at his beard and rushed forward crying, 'Give the devil the lie!' So our men fell upon the enemy, who retreated back up the hill. When I saw the Franks flying, I cried out with glee, 'Ah, we have routed them!' But they charged again and drove our troops back to where my father was standing. Again he urged them forward; again they drove the enemy back up the hill; again I cried out, 'We have routed them!' But my father turned to me impatiently and said, 'Be quiet. We have not beaten them so long as that red tent still stands.' At that moment the tent was overturned. Then my faher bowed to the ground and, with tears of joy, gave thanks to Allah."

The Horns of Hattin was an unparalleled disaster for the kingdom of Jerusalem. Nearly every man of fighting age was either killed or taken prisoner and sold into slavery. Only the very old and the very young were left to defend the kingdom, and they were not enough. The Moslem army moved at will throughout the country, and one by one Saladin conquered the towns and cities and fortresses. In October 1187 he recaptured Jerusalem itself, along with the True Cross, the holiest relic in Christendom. Saladin was a merciful conqueror (unlike Godfrey of Bouillon and his Crusaders, who had slaughtered almost the entire Moslem and Jewish population of the city). He allowed the women and children to go free and did not desecrate the Christian churches and shrines. But he sprinkled the mosques with rose water to cleanse them, dedicated them anew to the service of Allah, and once again the wailing cry of the muezzin was heard, calling the faithful to prayer in the city that is holy to Christians, Moslems, and Jews.

All that remained of the kingdom of Jerusalem was the port of Tyre, in present-day Lebanon. It still held out under the leadership of a recently arrived Crusader named Conrad of Montferrat, a cousin of Philip Augustus.

When word of the disaster reached Europe, the aged pope, Urban III, died of grief. His successor sent emissaries fanning out across the continent to preach a new Crusade. First to "take the cross" and set out with his army for the Holy Land was Emperor Frederick Barbarossa of Germany, who had also taken part in the Second Crusade forty years earlier. His expedition came to a sudden end at a little stream in Asia

Minor. Frederick, who had ridden ahead with his bodyguard, dismounted at the stream, bent over to drink, tripped on a rock and fell into the water. He was immediately dragged under by the weight of his armor, and before his men could pull him out, the seventy-year-old monarch had drowned. His Crusade at once collapsed. A few thousand Germans continued on to Tyre, where they later came under the command of Duke Leopold of Austria. The rest returned to their homes.

In the meantime, King Henry, Philip Augustus, Richard, and scores of lesser nobles had also taken the cross. Richard did not dare leave for the Holy Land until the question of his heritage had been settled. He knew that his father was perfectly capable of disinheriting him while he was away. So, early in 1189, he launched his rebellion.

This time, helped by the troops of Philip Augustus, Richard was unbeatable. Under his leadership, the combined forces of France and Aquitaine drove King Henry and his knights before them like cattle. On one occasion, just outside the town of Le Mans (Henry's birthplace), Richard almost captured his father. He was stopped at the last moment by William Marshal, who drove his lance into Richard's horse, bringing it to the ground.

But old King Henry was finished. He was so ill that he could hardly sit a horse, and his illness was aggravated when he learned that his adored son, John, had also betrayed him and was supporting Richard. "Now let things go as they will,"

Henry said when he was told about John. "I care no more for myself or for the world."

On July 4, 1189, at the Capitulation of Azay, Henry bought peace by surrendering some of his lands to Philip Augustus and by naming Richard his heir. Two days later he died—as much of a broken heart, it was said, as of illness. His last recorded words were: "Shame, shame on a conquered king." As often happened when a rich man died, his body was stripped of its clothing and jewels by his attendants, who fled into the countryside. A rough cloth was thrown over the king's face and he was carried to the Abbey of Fontrevault, the tomb of the Plantagenets, where he was buried two days later. Richard attended the funeral but showed no emotion except to shudder slightly when he saw the king's face, stained with blood around the nostrils from the hemorrhage that had killed him.

Immediately after the funeral, Richard called William Marshal to one side and said to him, "So, fair Sir Marshal, you were minded to slay me the other day. By God's teeth, that would have been a bad day's work!"

"Had I meant to kill you, my lord," William replied proudly, "I would not have killed your horse. My lance knows well its target."

"I bear you no malice," Richard said—and promptly sent William to England with instructions to free Queen Eleanor from captivity and to help her govern the kingdom until he himself arrived.

A month later, on August 13, 1189, Richard landed at Portsmouth. Except for two brief visits, it was the first time he had touched English soil since he had been born. From Portsmouth he went to Winchester, where he was joined by his mother, and then on to London. Enthusiastic crowds lined the route, shouting, "Hurrah for Richard!" and "Long live the king!" Richard was now thirty-two years old and at the height of his powers: six feet three inches tall, with powerful arms and shoulders, a deep chest, and the regal bearing of a man born to rule. He was "every inch a king, the idol of dames and damsels, who sighed to see him pass." It made no difference that he spoke hardly any English, for England was governed by the descendants of William the Conqueror and his Norman nobles, who had invaded the island in 1066, and French was still the everyday language of these people.

The coronation took place on Sunday, September 3, 1189. It was a splendid ceremony, which set the standard for all subsequent coronations. Richard, wearing gorgeous robes of silver and blue, walked from Westminster Palace to Westminster Abbey under a silken canopy that was held over his head by four barons. He was preceded and followed by the most powerful earls in the realm. One earl carried the cap of state, another the golden scepter surmounted by a golden cross, another the golden staff with a golden dove at its end, still another the great golden crown studded with rich gems.

Inside the abbey Richard stripped to his shirt and drawers, put on gold-embroidered slippers, and knelt at the altar. Archbishop Baldwin of Canterbury anointed him with oil on the head, shoulders, and chest. As this was being done, a bat suddenly swooped down from the ceiling, flew around the kneeling king, and vanished once more into the shadows. Superstitious nobles in the audience gasped and called it an evil omen, but Richard only smiled.

Then Richard was brought a copy of the Gospels and a jeweled coffer which contained the relics of many saints. On these holy objects he swore the triple oath: that all the days of his life he would show peace and honor and reverence to God and the Holy Church and the clergy; that he would exercise right justice over the people committed to his rule; and that he would blot out all evil laws and wrongful customs, if any existed in his realm, and would preserve good laws and customs. Then he was dressed in royal robes; the archbishop put the scepter in his right hand and the verge in his left; two earls held the crown over his head (for it was too heavy to wear); and he sat down on the marble throne.

Now, as King Richard I of England, the most powerful monarch in Christendom, he was ready at last to embark on the great adventure of his life—the Crusade.

THE THIRD CRUSADE BEGINS

3

IN HIS OUTLOOK and customs, as well as in his speech, Richard was French rather than English. He regarded England only as a place in which to raise money to finance his foreign adventures. "I would sell London itself if I could find a bidder," he was heard to say shortly after his coronation.

To pay for the Crusade, Richard all but stripped England of its wealth. "Everything was for sale," wrote Roger of Hoveden, "privileges, lordships, earldoms, sheriffdoms, castles, towns, and suchlike. . . . He relieved all those whose money was a burden to them."

Richard continued the "Saladin Tithe," which King Henry had declared when he took the cross. By its terms all the Jews in England were taxed twenty-five per cent of everything they owned, and the Christians ten per cent of their movable property. Anti-Semitic riots broke out in a number of cities, for it was rumored that the new king had ordered all Jews to be killed and their property confiscated. Nearly a hundred Jews were killed in London, and much of the Jewry (ghetto) was burned to the ground. The worst outbreak took place in York, where one of Richard's bastard half-brothers was archbishop. About a thousand Jews, including many women and children, shut themselves up in the castle and defended it against the mob. The Christians brought up siege engines, however, against which the Jews had no defense. Rather than be tortured and massacred, the Jewish men killed their wives and children and then each other. Only a handful were still alive the next morning, when the Christians broke into the castle, and they were quickly slaughtered.

But Richard, like his father, protected the Jews in his domains. He put a stop to the riots, had three of the ringleaders hanged, and even allowed one Jew, who had become a Christian in order to stay alive, to rejoin his religion. Archbishop Baldwin then remarked about the Jew: "If he won't be God's man, he had better be the Devil's."

In addition to the Saladin Tithe, Richard sold charters to a number of towns, granting them the right to raise their own taxes and manage their own affairs, like some of the so-called "free cities" on the continent. He sold to barons and lesser nobles the right to hunt in the royal forests and the right to hold tournaments. He forced the widow of the Earl of Essex, an enormously wealthy woman, to marry a poor knight named William de Forz, who showed his gratitude to the king by later donating a large sum to the king's coffers. Richard's justiciar, William Longchamp, also "took for the king's use from every city and town in England, two palfreys and two sumpter [pack] horses, as well as *huissiers, esneccae,* and *busses.*" (*Hussiers* were small, round-shaped sailing vessels; *esneccae* were fishing smacks; and *busses* were great ships of burden.) Richard also collected a number of speedy war galleys and put them under the command of Admiral Alan Trenchmer. Each galley was equipped with two banks of oars, a "castle" fore and aft, and a sharp spur in the prow for ramming. These vessels all gathered at the ports in southeast England and gradually filled up with knights and sergeants who came streaming along the roads from every corner of the kingdom. Barrels of meat and grain were loaded aboard, as well as sacks of biscuits and leather "hoses" of wine and water that were shaped like boots but closed at the top. To enforce discipline in his army, Richard had a copy of the King's Charter nailed to the mast of every tenth vessel. The Charter read:

"Richard, by the grace of God King of England, Duke of Normandy and Aquitaine, and Count of Anjou, to all his men who are about to journey to Jerusalem by sea—health. Know that with the common counsel of approved men we have had the following rules drawn up. Whoever on board ship shall slay another is himself to be cast into the sea lashed to the dead man. If he have slain him ashore, he is to be buried in the same way. If anyone be proved by worthy witnesses to have drawn a knife for the purpose of striking another, or to have wounded so as to draw blood, let him loose his fist; but if he strikes another with his hand and draw no blood, let him be dipped three times in the sea. If anyone cast any reproach or bad word against another, or call down God's curse upon him, let him for every offense pay an ounce of silver. Let a convicted thief be shorn like a prize-fighter, after which let boiling pitch be poured on his head and a feather pillow shaken over it so as to make him a laughingstock. Then let him be put ashore at the first land where the ships touch."

Richard himself suffered too much from seasickness to travel by ship except when he had no choice. In fact the sole job of one of his staff, the Grand Sergeant, was to hold the king's head while he vomited over the rail. So, on a fine, calm day in December, after spending only four months in England, he sped across the Channel in his galley and continued his preparations in Normandy and Aquitaine—pausing on the way south to storm the castle of a robber baron named Chis of Bigorre and to hang him from the walls.

Richard's English subjects were sorry to see him go. "As the earth grows dark when the sun departs," wrote Richard of Devizes, "so the face of the kingdom was changed by the absence of the king. All the barons were disturbed, castles were strengthened, towns fortified, ditches dug." The barons made these warlike preparations because Richard had left the power in England divided between his brother John and his chief justiciar William Longchamp. These two men despised each other and were already preparing a struggle for supremacy. Indeed, John's followers openly referred to him as "the next king."

Meanwhile Philip Augustus had also been busy raising an army. In July 1190 he and Richard met in the little town of Vézelay, which was famous as the place where Saint Bernard of Clairvaux had preached the Second Crusade to Philip's father. They spent a few days there and then set off, side by side, through the fields and vineyards of Burgundy, laughing

and chatting as if they were going to a tournament rather than on a campaign from which they might easily not return. Philip was accompanied by almost his entire army—flags and banners flying, the French wearing large red crosses sewed to their surcoats, the men from Flanders and Lorraine wearing green crosses. Richard's force of English, Norman, and Aquitainian knights and sergeants wore white crosses. Since Crusaders were under the Church's protection, none of them wore armor or carried weapons. Weapons and armor followed behind in wagons or on sumpter horses, along with the siege engines, victuals, and other items.

At Lyons there was a minor disaster when the bridge over the Rhône collapsed and a number of English men-at-arms

fell into the river and drowned. The crossing was finished in
boats and on rafts, and then the two groups separated. Philip
continued with his men to Genoa, Italy, where a fleet of
Genoese ships awaited him, and Richard followed the Rhône
Valley down to Marseilles, where he had arranged to be
picked up by his ships from England. Before parting, the two
kings agreed to meet in Messina, Sicily, where they would
spend the winter before going on to the Holy Land. It was the
last time they talked together as friends.

Trouble started in September, soon after Richard's fleet
of about a hundred vessels sailed into the harbor at Messina.
Philip and his men were already there and had taken the best
quarters available. Philip was lodged in a splendid palace
and his men in comfortable houses within the city's walls.
Richard had to be content with a cottage in the suburbs, and
his knights with a mosquito-infested campsite near the beach.
This annoyed both the king and his men, who felt they were
being slighted.

Richard also had other, more personal reasons, for being
annoyed. Sicily was ruled by a Norman adventurer named
Tancred, an ugly little man who had taken power on the
death of the island's last king, William the Good. William
had been married to Richard's favorite sister, Joanna, and on
his death bed he had bequeathed his father-in-law, Henry II,

a legacy consisting of gold plate, gold furniture, a huge silk tent, two armed galleys, and many sacks of provisions. But when Tancred snatched the throne, he had imprisoned Joanna and confiscated William's legacy for himself. Richard now sent him a curt note, demanding both his sister and the legacy. Tancred, feeling safe in his capital of Catania, sent only Joanna, her "bedroom furniture," and a small sum of money for her expenses.

Nor did things go smoothly between Richard's troops and their Sicilian hosts. Both groups were at fault. The people of Messina—about half of whom were Italian and the other half Greek (nicknamed "Grifones" by the Crusaders)—looked down on Richard's men as ruffians from the West, over-charged them for food and drink, and in general made them feel unwelcome. For their part the Crusaders, living in miserable conditions near the beach, drank too much wine in the taverns and inns, quarreled with the Sicilians about the prices, and molested their wives and daughters.

Tension built up between the two groups until, on October 3, 1190, rioting broke out in a suburb and a number of men on each side were killed. A rumor spread that Richard intended to conquer Sicily, and the gates of Messina were closed against him and his men.

The next morning Philip Augustus and several of Tancred's

nobles went to Richard's cottage to discuss with him how to avoid further unpleasant incidents. The meeting was proceeding amicably when Richard was drawn to the window by an uproar in the streets. Rioting had broken out once more. Crusaders were being stoned and Sicilians were yelling, "Down with Richard! Death to the English!"

The king's wrath was so terrible, we are told, "that he frightened his nearest friends and no one dared to look him in the face." He strode outside, found his lieutenants, and ordered them to take the city by storm.

Richard's order was swiftly carried out. Crossbowmen sent a hail of bolts against the Sicilians stationed on top of the wall, driving them to seek shelter. Then a group of sergeants used a battering ram to smash open the western gate to the city. There was a crash of splintering wood and ten thousand furious Crusaders, Richard at their head, raced through the gate. Within a few hours the Plantagenet banner —displaying three leopards *passant* (horizontal), with bared claws and fangs—flew from the towers and battlements. The English troops careered drunkenly through the streets, looting houses, raping the women, and singing, "The King of England has taken Messines quicker than priests can chant the Matines."

Richard calmed down when Tancred sent him twenty thousand ounces of gold in lieu of William the Good's legacy.

He ordered his banners taken down and most of the booty restored. But to prevent any further trouble with the Sicilians, he took hostages from the leading citizens of Messina. He also built a squat wooden castle on a nearby hill and stocked it with catapults with which he could bombard the city if that should prove necessary. With grim humor he called the castle *Mategrifon* (Kill-Greek).

In addition to the twenty thousand ounces of gold, Tancred also sent Richard a letter that he claimed had been written to him by Philip Augustus. Richard flew into another rage when he read the letter, for it suggested that the French and Sicilians get together and attack the English in their camp.

Confronted with the letter, Philip denied having written it. It was a forgery, he scoffed, and had obviously been written by Tancred to stir up trouble between the French and the English. Moreover, he went on, Richard was only using the letter as an excuse to break off his engagement to Alice. Wasn't it true, Philip said, that Richard had proposed marriage to Berengaria of Navarre, even though he was still officially betrothed to Alice? And wasn't it true that Berengaria, chaperoned by Queen Eleanor, was even then on her way to Sicily to join her fiancé?

Richard, always better with weapons than with words, sullenly admitted the truth of Philip's accusation. He agreed to pay Alice a large sum for breach of promise, agreed that the letter was probably a forgery, and he and Philip exchanged the kiss of peace. The seeds of distrust had been planted, however, and the two monarchs were never again to be friends.

In March 1191 the French sailed to the Holy Land. They debarked at Tyre, joined forces with Conrad of Montferrat, and marched down the coast to besiege Acre, which, next to Jerusalem, was the most important city in the country. Richard and his army set sail a month later, on the Wednesday before Easter. His fleet had grown in size and now numbered about two hundred vessels. All of them, except the galleys, were square-rigged sailing ships, which could only go before the wind.

Richard had bad luck. Two days after sailing, on Good Friday, a storm blew up and scattered his fleet all over the eastern Mediterranean. Several ships went down with all aboard. Most of the rest found shelter in Crete. Six vessels, including one transport that carried Joanna and Berengaria, and another that held all of Richard's money, were blown to the port of Limassol on the island of Cyprus. Richard himself, in his galley, was driven by the wind to Rhodes. Although he was violently seasick, he remained calm and confident, even at the height of the storm. He relied upon the Gray (Cistercian) Monks to save them, he told his terrified sailors, for they had promised to pray for him daily. "And I have done them such great kindnesses that I cannot doubt that as soon as they begin to pray for me God will look down and pity us."

While Richard recuperated in Rhodes, light galleys under Admiral Trenchmer went out and rounded up the fleet. The admiral returned empty-handed from Cyprus, however, and had a disturbing tale to tell. The ruler of Cyprus, he said, a Byzantine named Isaac Comnenus, had pillaged four of the shipwrecked vessels, clapping the English sailors and soldiers into prison, and would not allow the two important ships to take on fresh water so that they could continue their journey.

Richard was in a grim mood when he sailed to Cyprus a few days later. He debarked his army a little way up the coast from Limassol and marched on the city. The defenders, fighting from behind a barricade of timber and furniture, were swiftly overwhelmed, and Isaac and his cavalry fled to the slopes of Mount Troodos. Richard, seeing him go, shouted, "Emperor! Emperor! Come and joust!" He threw himself onto a nearby plowhorse "with a sack attached to its saddle and stirrups of rope," drew his sword, and clattered helter-skelter after the emperor. But Isaac set spurs to his horse and galloped off.

During the afternoon the destriers were brought ashore and Richard, accompanied by about fifty knights, set out after Isaac. He caught up to the Cypriots just before nightfall, lined

up his men, and prepared to charge. "Come away, Sire," said a clerk who was with him, "their numbers are too overwhelming."

"Get you to your writing business, sir clerk," Richard replied, "and leave matters of chivalry to us." He lowered his lance and charged, followed by his knights. The lightly armed and armored Cypriots scattered in all directions, Isaac among them. The emperor rode the finest destrier Richard had ever seen, a big bay stallion named Fauvel. Time and again, while his pursuers cursed in frustration, Fauvel showed his heels to the swiftest mounts in Richard's army.

The king returned to Limassol and celebrated his easy victory by marrying Berengaria in the dim, tiny chapel of the Church of Saint George, which still stands. While the wedding feast was under way, messengers arrived from Isaac, asking for a parley. Richard, still wearing his bridegroom's rose-colored tunic, scarlet cap, and mantle covered with golden sunbursts and silver half-moons, mounted his black Spanish stallion and rode north to meet Isaac in a grove of fig trees by the sea. The parley came to nothing, for though Isaac swore fealty to Richard and agreed to take part in the Crusade, he broke his oath the next morning and ordered the

king to leave the island within two days or "face the conse-
quences of his folly."

Richard of course did not take Isaac's threat seriously, but
he had another problem. Cyprus was the closest point to
Palestine and would make a fine source of supplies for the
Crusaders, but he did not have enough men to undertake its
conquest. His problem was solved the next day, when several
galleys arrived from the Holy Land. They brought Guy of
Lusignan, who had been released by Saladin some time before, and many of his knights and men-at-arms. Guy had
come to seek Richard's support in a quarrel with Conrad of
Montferrat, who now claimed the throne of Jerusalem. Guy
and Richard took an immediate liking to one another and became fast friends. In the next fifteen days their combined
forces chased Isaac from one end of Cyprus to the other, capturing all the important towns and castles in the process.

At length Isaac had nowhere left to run, and surrendered.
He asked only two things: that his life be spared, and that he
not be put in irons. Richard promised—and then had half a
barrel of English silver pennies melted down and forged into
fetters for Isaac's wrists and ankles. The ex-ruler of Cyprus
paid dearly for his greed. He was handed over to the Knights
Hospitaller and imprisoned in their fortress of Markab in
Tripoli. He died there three years later. His young daughter,
the "Damosel of Cyprus," was attached to Queen Joanna's

court to learn the western way of life. She later married a Flemish knight.

Richard spent another eighteen days in Cyprus. He ordered the Cypriot men to shave off their beards as a token of submission; he collected a vast store of treasure; and he put two Englishmen, Robert of Turnham and Richard of Camville, in temporary charge of the island and told them to organize a regular supply of meat and grain to be sent to the Holy Land. Then, with Fauvel on the deck of his ship, he embarked his army and set sail.

Cyprus had been a pleasant and highly profitable diversion but it was time he got on with the main business of the Crusade—the restoration of the kingdom of Jerusalem.

THE SIEGE OF ACRE

4

RICHARD had his first encounter with the Saracens on the morning of June 6, 1191, when his fleet overtook a three-masted Moslem vessel that was loaded with troops and provisions destined for the besieged garrison in Acre. The English ships, Richard's galley in the lead, swarmed around the larger vessel but were driven off by a blinding shower of stones and javelins.

Richard, bareheaded and conspicuous in the poop of his galley, was miraculously unhurt, though men on either side of him were transfixed by javelins. But the king was furious. "What!" he shouted. "Will you let that ship get off unharmed? Shame on you! You will deserve to be hanged!"

Stung by this reproach, some of his men leaped into the water, swam over to the enemy ship, and tied her rudder with ropes so that she would not answer to her helm. Then the galleys came alongside again and the Christian soldiers and sailors tried to board. They were unable to fight their way past the crowd of Turks that lined the decks of the enemy vessel, however, and after many of them had had their hands lopped off and had fallen back into their galleys, the English ships drew away once more.

Richard changed tactics. Urging his oarsmen to pull hard on their sweeps, he sent the iron beak of his galley crashing into the side of the Saracen vessel. Other galleys followed his example and soon water was pouring into the Moslem ship through a score of gaping holes. The ship began to list, and the Turkish captain, seeing there was no hope, opened the seacocks and helped sink her. Within a few minutes it was all over. The Christians pulled thirty or forty of the better-dressed Saracens from the water and held them for ransom. The rest they left to drown.

The victory, minor though it was, lifted the Crusaders' spirits. It was a good omen and seemed to bode well for the future of their expedition. Their cheerfulness evaporated two days later, however, when they waded ashore near Acre, for the city was far larger and more heavily fortified than any they had yet encountered.

Acre was built on a narrow spur of land that jutted into the Mediterranean like a parrot's head, with the harbor to the south, inside the sheltering curve of the beak. There was no possibility of attacking the city from the seaward side, for the seawall was flush to the rocky shore; and it was protected on the landward side by an L-shaped wall, nearly a hundred feet high and twenty feet thick, which ran across the neck of land from sea to sea. At the angle of the L stood "the Accursed Tower," as the Christians called it. From the top of this bastion the Saracens controlled all approaches to the wall and kept the besiegers at a respectful distance.

The Crusaders' camp formed a great semicircle along the shore, banners and pennants flying from the tops of the striped pyramidal tents, the sun winking from armor and weapons as the men polished them with sand and ashes. Historians were vague about figures in those days, but the entire "host" probably numbered thirty to forty thousand knights and sergeants, plus a few thousand women, children, priests, monks, and other noncombatants. They came from nearly every Christian country in Europe and, had they cooperated with each other, were numerous enough to have overwhelmed the city. Because of feuds and jealousy between the commanders, however, each national group kept to its own area and fought its own battles, independent of the others.

The critical position, opposite the Accursed Tower, was occupied by Philip Augustus, Conrad of Montferrat, and their men. To their north and south, respectively, were the Knights Templar and Richard's troops. South of Richard was Duke

Leopold of Austria with several thousand Germans, Austrians, Hungarians, and Scandinavians. Then came Guy of Lusignan and his *poulains* (Christians who had been born in the Holy Land). And on the extreme southern end were the Knights Hospitaller. Scattered among these groups, and also manning the blockading fleet, were men from the Italian maritime cities of Genoa, Venice, and Pisa—all deadly rivals who fought each other as readily as they fought the Saracens.

The Crusaders had thrown up earthwork ramparts on the inland side of the camp. These were intended to protect them against Saladin, who was entrenched in the nearby hills with a large force of Turkish and Arabic troops. Every time the Christians tried to storm the walls of Acre, Saladin attacked them in the rear, forcing them to defend their camp. The besiegers were being besieged.

Richard's arrival put new heart into the discouraged Crusaders. Bonfires were lighted and trumpets sounded to celebrate his landing. "Then," wrote the historian Ernoul, who was there, "did the Christians gird up their loins, and smile, and swear that the Infidel would feel the might of Christian arms."

But Richard was not yet the overall commander of the Crusade. That honor still belonged to the King of France, both by tradition and because he had the largest army. Within hours after Richard's arrival, he and Philip quarreled once more. The ostensible cause of the quarrel was Richard's refusal to give Philip half of Cyprus. The real cause, however, was Philip's envy of the effortless way in which Richard inspired the admiration and devotion of his followers. Philip had been born a king, while Richard had been born a magnetic leader of men as well. After the quarrel the two monarchs were not only no longer friends: they were deadly enemies.

Richard was disgusted by the way Philip was conducting the siege. The only way to take a well-fortified city like Acre, as he knew from experience, was to move in close. Then, while the archers and crossbowmen swept the garrison from the top of the wall with their arrows and bolts, the engineers could mine beneath it or the sergeants could move up with their picks and pry loose stone after stone until a breach had been opened and the waiting knights could pour into the city and take it by storm.

None of this was happening, partly because of Philip's timidity and partly because of a fearsome Saracen weapon—earthenware jars filled with a colorless inflammable liquid, probably naphtha, with a wick of flaming cloth tied to the handle of each jar. Saracen catapults hurled the jars from within the city and from the top of the Accursed Tower. They shattered on impact and burst immediately into flames of such intensity that no one could approach them. Many of the Crusaders' small catapults had gone up in smoke, while their two giant boulder-throwing mangonels—"The Evil Neighbor" and "God's Own Sling"—were spared only because they were kept out of range.

After puzzling about them for some time, the French engineers thought they had found the answer to the jars. They built a huge wooden tower, taller than the wall, and, to make it fireproof, they draped it all over with the hides of freshly slaughtered animals. It was by means of just such a tower that Godfrey of Bouillon had taken Jerusalem in 1099.

A picked group of knights climbed to the upper level of the tower, another group to the level below, and hundreds of men-at-arms put their shoulders to the framework and began rolling it forward on logs which had been stripped of their bark.

As the hide-draped tower creaked slowly toward the wall, jar after jar flew through the air and shattered against it. But these jars had no flaming wicks attached to them, so the liquid only soaked into the wood and dripped from the hides. The French in the tower began to cheer. Success seemed within their grasp. They drew their swords and prepared to leap onto the wall.

But suddenly, when the tower was only a short distance from its goal, a blazing tree trunk sailed over the wall and landed at its feet with a shower of sparks. For a moment nothing happened. Then, with a muffled roar, white flames leaped up and the trapped knights began to cry out in agony.

Three of them escaped by jumping to the ground and running back to their lines. The rest were burned alive.

King Philip, who was watching the assault from a safe distance, "began to curse with horrid oaths at all who were under his rule, and to chide them with shameful reproaches for not taking vengeance against the Saracens who had done him such a wrong." In his fury, he sent heralds throughout the French camp to proclaim a general assault for the next day.

This attack failed also. At the crucial moment Saladin launched his Turks against the camp and the Crusaders were forced onto the defensive. Although there was bitter fighting, the camp was never in danger of being overrun. "The Franks showed all the weakness of a stone wall," wrote the Arab chronicler, Beha-ed-Din. "One gigantic knight climbed upon the earthwork parapet and held off a Moslem division all by himself. His comrades passed up boulders to him which he hurled down on our men. He was hit by more than twenty arrows and stones but did not seem to notice them. Finally, one of our officers smashed a fire pot against his armor and burned him alive."

Soon after this failure both Richard and Philip came down with what the chroniclers called *arnaldia*—a type of fever, probably malaria, that was raging in the Christian ranks. More than a thousand Crusaders, including the count of Flanders and other important nobles, had already died of the disease, and thousands of others lay shivering and sweating in their tents. Philip's hair and nails fell out, he grew terrified of dying, and he began to speak of abandoning the Crusade and returning to France. Richard reacted differently. Although he was seriously ill, he had his litter carried to the front line and took command of the siege.

Under his inspired leadership, the tempo of the attack increased day by day. The mangonels kept up a steady bombardment, hurling particularly hard boulders that Richard had brought with him from Sicily. One of these boulders shattered on top of the wall and the flying splinters killed twelve Saracens. Saladin had bits of the stone brought to him, for he was always interested in military matters. The sultan greatly admired Richard, both for his fighting prowess and for his chivalry. "If I must lose the Holy City," he said to Beha-ed-Din, "I would rather lose it to that man than to any other Nazarene in all the world." Indeed, Saladin so admired his adversary that he is supposed to have sent him bowls of fresh fruit, packed in snow from Mount Hermon, to help him recover from his illness.

While the mangonels and crossbowmen made life miserable for the defenders, Richard's engineers mined beneath the Accursed Tower, propping up the roof of the tunnel with beams soaked in pitch. On the afternoon of July 3, 1191, while Richard watched from his litter, the engineers set fire to the beams and scuttled out of the tunnel.

The mine failed to do its job, however. The beams burned

through, the tunnel collapsed, but the Accursed Tower only lurched forward and then settled at an angle—damaged but still intact.

"God's feet!" Richard roared, glaring at his engineers. But for once the king reined his temper. He shouted to his men, offering a gold piece for every stone they ripped from the tower. The Crusaders hesitated, for Saracen archers now lined the battlements. Two gold pieces, Richard cried. At this, the men quickly raised a testudo, or tortoise shell of shields, over their heads and rushed forward with picks and crowbars. On two gold pieces, a family could live comfortably in England for six months.

All afternoon and the following night the men clawed at the tower, picking loose the mortar and prying out the great stone blocks. The Saracens shot arrows at them, poured cauldrons of boiling water or oil on their heads, and hundreds of the Crusaders were killed or wounded. But no sooner did one man fall than another moved up to take his place.

At last, shortly after sunrise, a section of the tower came crashing down. The knights and sergeants raced forward crying "*Christus vincit!*—Christ victorious!" and began clambering up the mound of rubble to the breach. First to reach the top was a Norman knight named Alberic Clements, who had sworn to get into Acre that day or die. The men behind Clements saw him sihouetted against the sky, waving his sword and shouting. Then he went down, "pierced with countless wounds."

There was a moment of fierce hand-to-hand fighting in the breach, then fire pots began to land on the rubble, setting fire to the clothing of Saracens and Christians alike. The Crusaders dropped their weapons and fled, beating out their blazing garments. The Accursed Tower had been breached, but Acre still held.

The defenders, however, were in a bad way. They were short of food, short of arrows, and they were nearly out of liquid for the fire pots. That night one of the garrison swam ashore, made his way to Saladin's tent, and explained the situation. Unless the sultan could lift the siege within a day or two, he concluded, the city would have to surrender.

Saladin was horrified. The conquest of Acre would give the Christians a secure foothold in the Holy Land once more. So the next morning he launched a desperate attack, led by his nephew Taki, against the camp. It was beaten off with heavy Turkish losses, and a few days later, on Friday, July 11, 1191, the gates of Acre swung open and the remaining three thousand members of the garrison marched out into captivity. "We saw the Cross and the banners of the Franks appear on the walls," wrote the historian Abu Shama, who was standing beside Saladin. "An immense roar of joy rose from the Christian ranks—while we gnashed our teeth and wept with rage and humiliation. Oh, it was hateful to see Conrad of Montferrat enter the city with the flags of the four Christian kings and plant them one by one on the citadel and on the minaret of the grand mosque!"

The four kings were Philip, Richard, Guy, and Conrad. Duke Leopold of Austria tried to claim equal status with them by planting his flag next to theirs, but Richard publicly insulted him and had his flag thrown down and trampled into the dust. When Leopold left for Austria shortly afterward, it was with a hatred of Richard in his heart. He was to take his revenge later.

According to the terms of the surrender, the lives of the Moslem garrison would be spared if Saladin returned the True Cross, released sixteen hundred Christian prisoners from the dungeons in Aleppo and Damascus, and paid a ransom of two hundred thousand gold pieces. The sultan was given a month to meet these terms.

Meanwhile the Crusaders prepared for the march south to the port of Jaffa, their next objective. All day the clang of metal on metal was heard as armorers beat out the dents in helmets, replaced broken links in chain mail, sharpened swords and lance points. Ships plied back and forth from Cyprus, bringing supplies of meat and grain, as well as destriers to replace those which had been killed. The Accursed

Tower was rebuilt and the walls repaired. The mosques were reconsecrated as churches, and priests said special masses in them for the Crusaders who had died during the siege.

Philip Augustus, still not recovered from his illness, departed from France. To compensate for breaking his Crusader's vows in this way, he left behind ten thousand men under the Duke of Burgundy. He also swore not to attack Normandy or Aquitaine during Richard's absence. "How faithfully he kept this oath," drily comments an English chronicler, "all the world knows."

Saladin's time limit of a month elapsed, was extended, elapsed again, and still the sultan made no move to comply with the terms of the surrender. Richard fretted and walked around with a perpetual scowl on his handsome features. He was anxious to be on the move, but first he had to deal with the Moslem prisoners. He could not take them with him; he could not set them free to fight again; and he could not keep them locked up indefinitely. To his harsh medieval mind, there was only one solution.

On the morning of August 20, when Saladin's last time limit expired, the entire Crusading army marched out of Acre and formed up in battle array on the inland slope of a hill known ever since as the "Hill of the Martyrs." Saladin's men hastily armed themselves, anticipating an attack, but the Crusaders remained motionless. Then the Saracens saw a column of Moslem prisoners, roped together and with their hands tied behind their backs, herded along to the top of the hill. Saladin saw what was about to happen and ordered his Turkish cavalry to mount and try to rescue the prisoners.

The galloping Saracens were still several hundred yards away, however, when Richard raised his sword overhead and brought it down in a sweeping gesture. At his signal the Crusaders rushed upon the helpless prisoners and cut them down, thanking God for the chance to avenge their dead comrades. Within a few moments nearly three thousand Moslems lay sprawled upon the hill, their life's blood soaking into the sandy soil.

Saladin's horsemen, howling for vengeance, hurled themselves again and again upon the Crusaders, and were thrown back each time. At length they retired, and the Crusaders marched back into Acre.

"And there was no sign from heaven," wrote a later historian, "nothing to show that a Crusade so begun could never succeed. . . . Richard's hands were stained."

THE ROAD TO JERUSALEM
5

TWO DAYS after the massacre, on August 22, 1191, the Crusaders started south along the coast toward Jaffa, the port for Jerusalem. The men grumbled at first, for, as a monk named Ambroise wrote, "They were reluctant to leave the delights of Acre, whose taverns were overflowing with wine and women. . . . By King Richard's order, no prostitutes made this journey. The only women allowed to follow the troops were those old raddled creatures who washed the laundry and the soldiers' heads, and who, for picking lice and fleas from the hair, were as good as monkeys."

Ambroise and the other chroniclers paint a clear picture of the Crusading army as it plowed slowly along the beach, past patches of scrub oak and stone pine, with the scent of thyme and rosemary wafting down from the hills. The host marched in three columns: the baggage wagons and sumpter horses on the right, closest to the sea; the mounted knights and squires on their left; and inland, forming a protective hedge against Saladin's men, who kept pace among the hills, came the foot soldiers. Richard himself, his chain mail gleaming like silk in the sun, roved between the head and the tail of the army, urging the stragglers forward, encouraging his troops with promises of loot and glory.

The Moslems rode close herd on the Christians. At least once a day bands of Saracen cavalry would sweep down from the hills crying, *"Allahu akbar!"* ("Allah is most great!"), darken the sky with volleys of arrows, and race away again before the knights, on their larger and clumsier mounts, could organize a pursuit.

These attacks were effective only against the horses. "The Frankish infantry," wrote the Arab chronicler, el-Imad, "wore felt corsets which were so tightly woven that our arrows could not penetrate them. I myself saw one soldier trudging along unconcerned with ten arrows planted in his back."

A more dangerous enemy was the heat. The midsummer sun blazed pitilessly down, and many knights, sweltering in their quilted *gambesons* (undergarments that prevented the armor from chafing), their hauberks of chain mail and their heavy iron helmets, collapsed and died of sunstroke or heat exhaustion. Richard grew so alarmed at the number of knights who died in this way that he began to halt the army for several hours in the middle of the day. During these rest periods, while the men sprawled in whatever shade they could find,

priests and monks moved among them, doling out water and crying, *"Sanctum Sepulchrum adjuva!"* (Help us, Holy Sepulchre!"). The knights and sergeants, writes a chronicler, took up the cry, "stretching out their hands to heaven and, with copious tears, praying God for aid and mercy."

Saladin had lost prestige at Acre and was determined to regain it by forcing a battle. He gradually increased the pressure on the Christians until, on a narrow plain just north of the village of Arsuf, he blocked the road. The Crusaders were cut off on three sides, had their backs to the sea, and were outnumbered at least five or six to one. To the pessimists among them, it looked as though another disaster similar to Hattin was in the making.

But Richard was not dismayed. When he saw that a battle was inevitable, he placed the archers and pikemen in the front rank, with the mounted men behind them. The Templars held the right flank, next to the sea; the Hospitallers the left flank. Richard himself occupied the center with his English and French knights. He rode up and down the line, shouting words of encouragement to his men and ordering that in no circumstances were they to attack before the trumpeters sounded the charge.

The Saracens launched their assault in the middle of the morning. Ambroise, observing the action from the wagon that carried Richard's leopard standard, has left us a wonderful account of the battle:

"First came the trumpeters and drummers, sounding their instruments and yelling so loudly that God himself would not have been heard. Then they moved away and wave after wave of Negro and Bedouin infantry raced forward, shooting their arrows and letting fly with their spears. They threw the first line of our infantry into disorder but made no impression upon the men of iron behind them. Then the Turkish cavalry, their axes and sabres flashing in the sunlight, charged the Knights of the Hospital, hoping to turn our left flank, and you could see nothing in the turmoil of dust, shrieking horses and shouting men."

The Hospitallers held firm, though nearly half their horses were killed. The Grand Master of the Order galloped up to Richard and begged for permission to attack. His knights, he said, were not used to playing the coward's role; unless they could take the offensive, they would have to yield.

"Patience, my good Master," Richard told him. "Another few minutes—when their main army is closer."

But just then a Hospitaller named Baldwin Carew put the spurs to his destrier, cried, "For Christ and Saint George!" and galloped headlong toward the Saracens. His charge was infectious and soon the whole line of knights was in motion. "The Hospitallers," wrote Ambroise, "charged in good order and were followed by Count Henry of Champagne and his brave companions, and Count James of Avesnes and his followers. Count Robert of Dreux and the Bishop of Beauvais

charged together. From the right, by the sea, charged the
Earl of Leicester with all his men, and there were no cowards
among them. Then all the army was charging—the Angevins,
the Poitevins, the Bretons, the Manceaux, the Normans, the
English, and all the other divisions. Oh, the brave knights!
They attacked the Turks with such vigor that each one found
his man, planted his lance in his entrails, and hurled him from
the stirrups. . . . When King Richard saw that the charge
had begun without waiting for his command, he clapped his
heels into Fauvel's flanks and launched himself at full speed
against the enemy. And such was his prowess on that September day before Arsuf that all around him I saw the bodies of
Turks with their bearded heads planted like cabbages in the
field."

The magnificent charge, which made Saladin gasp with
admiration, was too much for the Saracens, and they broke
and fled. The Crusaders chased them more than a mile inland,
to the slope of a hill covered with scrub oak. Some of the
Saracens climbed up the taller trees and clung to the branches,
yelling for mercy—only to be shot down by the archers.

But the battle was not yet over. The Saracens could see that
the Christians had broken formation and were scattered all
over the field in little groups, their horses' flanks coated with
lather and they themselves drooping wearily in the saddle.
They appeared less formidable now, and a number of Turkish

emirs, waving their yellow and green and red silk banners in the air, rallied their men and swarmed down the hill to wipe out their disgrace.

When Richard saw what was happening, he gathered his personal bodyguard of twenty knights and raced into action. He and his men fought their way through to one group of beleagured knights after another, joined them together, and then, when a large enough force had been assembled, led them in another charge. This one was decisive. The Saracens rallied in time to protect the sultan's tent but abandoned the field to the Christians. Once again the "men of iron from the West" were a force to be reckoned with, and Hattin had been avenged.

Although Saladin's army was still intact, still capable of taking the field against the Christians, the sultan was too wily to risk another pitched battle. Instead, he resorted to "scorched earth" tactics, moving rapidly down the coast in advance of the Crusaders and destroying one town and fortress after another. In quick succession he evacuated the Moslems from Caesarea, Jaffa, and Ascalon, emptied their granaries, drove their herds of livestock into Egypt, and burned their unharvested crops. Then he tore down their walls and towers and withdrew to the hills near Jerusalem to await Richard's next move.

Richard did not dare to march inland without a secure base on the coast, so he set his men to work rebuilding Jaffa's defenses. In the meantime he tried to negotiate a treaty with Saladin's younger brother, a handsome, high-spirited warrior named el-Adil. To the outrage and indignation of the more fanatical Crusaders, el-Adil and Richard became friends. They went hunting together with falcons on their wrists. They feasted together in the silk tent that had formerly belonged to Isaac Comnenus and were entertained by Bedouin dancers and Syrian jugglers. They exchanged gifts, and they made proposals and counterproposals.

The peace talks failed, however, for Saladin rejected all of Richard's proposals. As a last resort, Richard offered to give his sister Joanna to el-Adil in marriage. If Saladin would return Jerusalem to the Christians, Richard said, he would give Joanna a dowry of all the Christian towns and fortresses along the coast, and she and el-Adil could thus rule a united country. The plan seemed promising, but it fell through when Joanna indignantly refused to consider marriage to an infidel. And so, at the end of October, el-Adil said goodbye to Richard and rode away to join his brother.

Early in December the work in Jaffa was finished, and Richard formed up the army and started inland toward the Holy City. The weather turned bad. Strong winds blew in from the sea and icy rain fell day after day. The rain turned the dusty mountain tracks into slippery morasses of ankle-deep mud; it spoiled the stores of pork and biscuits; and it made the men shiver with cold as they had shivered with malaria during the siege of Acre. To add to the Crusaders' difficulties, Saracen guerrillas swooped down upon the column from time to time and picked off stragglers. The Christians killed in these raids were luckier than those who were taken prisoner. Since the massacre of the garrison at Acre, the Saracens had tortured to death all Christians who fell into their hands. For their part, the Crusaders collected Moslem heads as Red Indians collected scalps. Like their barbarian ancestors, they hung the heads from their horses' bridles.

The Crusaders pressed steadily on, aflame with zeal to restore "God's own city" to Christendom. On January 3, 1192, they reached the fortress of Beit Nuba, only twelve miles from the Holy City. From the top of a nearby hill they could see the domes and minarets of Jerusalem, and the famous Mosque of Omar gleaming whitely in the distance; the sick and the lame Crusaders cried out that Christ's presence had already cured them. Richard was one of the first to climb the hill, but quickly raised his shield before his eyes. He had vowed not to look upon the Holy City until he was ready to deliver it from the infidel.

On January 6, Richard and his leading nobles held a council of war. A *poulain*, formerly a resident of Jerusalem, sketched a map of the city, indicating the walls and towers, Mount Zion, the valley of Kidron, and other geographical features which made it a difficult place to conquer. Richard brooded over the map for a long time. He already knew that Saladin had received reinforcements from Egypt and that the garrison in Jerusalem was composed of tough fighting men from Turkistan, on the southern border of Russia.

The French and English nobles were eager to begin the siege. They were confident that zeal alone was enough to solve all the problems. But Guy of Lusignan and the Grand Masters of the Templars and the Hospitallers advised against it. "Even if we took the city," Guy said to Richard, "we could not hold it. Your men would have fulfilled their Crusaders' vows and returned to their homes, and the might of united Islam would soon overwhelm us."

"Not so," said the Duke of Burgundy. "When word of our great victory reached Christendom, thousands of knights would take the cross and come to defend the Holy City."

The French and the *poulains* began to argue. The argument grew heated and they had nearly come to blows, when Richard waved them to silence. "Guy is right," he said, with tears in his eyes. "It will be impossible to take this town so long as Saladin lives and the Moslems are at peace with each other." Then, heaving a great sigh, he rose and gave orders to march back to the coast.

The retreat shattered the Crusaders' morale. To have seen the Holy City and not reconquer it was more than they could bear. The Duke of Burgundy and most of the French slipped away to Acre and refused to help Richard rebuild the fortress of Ascalon as he had rebuilt Jaffa. They were fighting men, they said, not stonemasons. The remaining Crusaders did all the work, turning Ascalon into the strongest fortress on the coast; but they complained unceasingly about the weather, about the bad food, and about the fact that they had not been paid in many months (for Richard's treasury was empty).

Another cause of dissension was the continuing quarrel between Conrad of Montferrat and Guy of Lusignan. Each claimed to be king of Jerusalem; each was backed by part of the army. To settle the quarrel once and for all, Richard called a conference of the leading nobles and asked them to choose between the two men. Richard himself favored his friend and countryman, Guy, but the nobles chose Conrad, because Guy's reputation was irrevocably stained by the defeat at the Horns of Hattin. To compensate Guy, Richard sold him Cyprus, thus founding the "House of Lusignan," which ruled the island for more than three centuries.

Conrad was in Acre when he learned of the nobles' decision. Falling to his knees, he cried out in a loud voice: "Oh, God, hear me! If I am unworthy of the crown, then give it to another!" A few days later, as he was returning from a visit to the Bishop of Beauvais's house, he was stopped in the street by two men dressed as monks. One of the monks handed him a letter. As he began to read it, the other drew a knife from his

robes and plunged it repeatedly into Conrad's belly and side.
Conrad was carried to his palace, where he died shortly afterward. One of his killers was hacked to death on the spot; the
other was taken prisoner, tortured, and confessed that he had
been sent to murder Conrad by the Old Man of the Mountains,
the leader of a fanatical Moslem sect called the Assassins.
(The name comes from *hashishiyun*, "hashish," which the
members of the sect ate or smoked before they set out on a
mission.) The Old Man of the Mountains had ordered the
murder because, several weeks earlier, Conrad had captured

a vessel loaded with goods bound for the Assassins and had refused to return it.

Two days after the murder, Conrad's young widow, Isabel, was betrothed to Richard's nephew, Count Henry of Champagne, and a few weeks after their marriage, Henry became king of Jerusalem. Although Henry was a handsome and popular young man, some of the men who had followed Conrad were dissatisfied. They suspected Richard of having connived at Conrad's murder so that his nephew would get the crown. This unfounded and far-fetched rumor was scoffed at by most of the troops, but a few of the French believed it and sailed for home, thus further depleting Richard's forces.

Richard was beset with other problems also. About the time that Conrad was killed, a priest arrived from England with news that Prince John had seized the royal treasury, driven the chief justiciar, William Longchamp, out of the country, and with the help of Philip Augustus was plotting to set himself up as King of England.

This news upset not only Richard (for he loved his brother and hated to think him capable of such treachery) but the Crusaders as well. With so much trouble at home, they said, the king would surely abandon the Crusade and return to England. Richard put an end to this defeatist talk by calling a meeting of the commanders and announcing publicly that "not for any messenger or evil tidings, nor for any earthly quarrel, would he depart from them or quit the land before next Easter."

Easter came and went, and still Richard lingered on the coast, waiting for the situation to change in his favor. At last, early in June, he formed up his sadly reduced army and marched inland again as far as Beit Nuba. He stayed there for three weeks, skirmishing with Saladin's troops but making no attempt to march on the Holy City. Not only was he faced with the same problems he had faced during the previous December, but Saladin had created a new one. The sultan had poisoned all the wells and cisterns for miles around Jerusalem, forcing Richard to send armed convoys nearly as far as the coast for barrels of water. Under such conditions, Richard knew, a successful siege would be impossible, and on July 3 he turned back to the coast once more.

This second retreat destroyed what remained of the Christians' morale and they deserted in droves. The Crusade would probably have ended then and there if an unexpected opportunity for booty had not presented itself.

Richard was still on the road to Jaffa when a spy brought word that a rich Moslem caravan, crossing from Egypt to Jerusalem, was camped at the Round Cistern in the Negev desert. Quickly choosing five hundred of his best knights, the king led them in a rapid march south. The Crusaders rode hard all night, and at dawn, wrapped in burnooses so that their armor would not reflect the sun, they galloped full tilt into the sleeping camp. "As greyhounds chase rabbits," wrote Ambroise, "so our men chased the Saracens into the desert. And a mighty harvest was ours—long lines of camels and donkeys loaded with gold, silk, velvet, royal purple, bowls and goblets of copper, silver candlesticks, Damascene armor, ivory chessmen, bales of sugar, pepper, frankincense, and foodstuffs—all the riches of Islam!"

The brilliant coup revived the Crusaders' flagging spirits and added luster to Richard's reputation, but it did nothing to change the basic situation. So long as Saladin lived and his army was intact, Jerusalem could not be attacked.

Back in Jaffa after the raid, Richard opened truce talks once more with Saladin's representatives. The talks progressed slowly as point by point was hammered out between the two monarchs. The sultan agreed to recognize Henry of Champagne as King of Jerusalem, to allow priests to conduct services in the Church of the Holy Sepulchre, to allow Christian pilgrims to visit Jerusalem, Nazareth, Bethlehem, and the other holy places. In return he demanded access to the ports of Acre and Jaffa, and he insisted that Ascalon be razed to the ground once more. Richard agreed to the first condition but balked at the second. At length, after haggling fruitlessly back and forth for several weeks, the king lost patience. He rode north with his followers, intending to make one last conquest—the port of Beirut in present-day Lebanon—and then sail for home.

This was the chance Saladin had been waiting for. No sooner had Richard left than the sultan moved his army down and besieged Jaffa. Within three days his catapults had battered a breach in the wall and the Saracen troops poured in and began slaughtering the populace. Soon all the city was theirs except for the citadel, where a few hundred Christians still held out.

When Saladin launched his attack, the commander of the garrison sent a messenger galloping north to Richard with a plea for help. "As God lives," the king said, "I will go there." While the bulk of his army marched overland, Richard sailed down the coast in galleys. He had with him fifty-five knights, four hundred men-at-arms, and about two thousand Genoese and Pisan marines.

Adverse winds delayed the fleet and when Richard finally reached Jaffa, it looked as though he were too late. Saracen banners fluttered from the towers and battlements, and the smoke of burning churches hung in a black pall over the city. Then the king, who was standing in the prow of his galley, saw a man sliding and scrambling down the wall of the citadel. The man—a priest—plunged into the sea and began swimming. A few Saracen arrows landed near him but he was picked up by a small boat and brought to Richard's galley.

"Is anyone left alive?" the king asked him.

"Yes," the priest replied. "In front of the citadel they are hemmed in and like to perish."

Richard ordered the galleys shoreward at once, and presently they grounded on the beach. Without taking time to put on armor, the king clapped a helmet on his head, grabbed a Danish battle-ax—a fearsome weapon, five feet long—and jumped into the shallow water. He waded ashore, shouting for his men to follow.

The Saracens were busy looting the city, so Richard took them by surprise. He raged through the streets "like a true lion," swinging his ax right and left and carving a bloody path to the citadel. There he was joined by the surviving members of the garrison and together they drove the Saracen from the city. Saladin tried to stem the retreat, but without success, and soon the entire Saracen army of nearly twenty thousand men was fleeing for the hills, chased by a Christian force less than one-tenth its size. "The king," wrote Ambroise, "covered with the caked dust and sweat of his exertions, erected his tent where Saladin's had stood a little while before. Never, not even at Roncesvalles where mighty Roland fought and died, did a paladin perform such glorious feats of arms as did our king that morning in Jaffa."

And from the Saracen viewpoint, Beha-ed-Din recorded Richard's mocking taunts to one of Saladin's emissaries who had come to reopen the parleys. "Your sultan," said Richard, "is the greatest ruler Islam ever had, and here my presence alone has made him decamp. As you can see, I am not even wearing armor, and on my feet are simple sailor's shoes. I did not come to fight. Why, then, has he fled?"

Richard's great victory, however, made him overconfident. Although his army was still a three-day march from Jaffa, he recklessly made camp outside the city's walls and did not bother to set men on watch. It was very nearly a disastrous mistake, for Saladin's rage and humiliation were unbounded and he was determined to crush the Crusaders with a surprise attack.

The Moslem army, reorganized and thirsting for vengeance, moved down on Jaffa during the night and was lined up in battle formation just before dawn. The attack would probably have succeeded if a Genoese sailor, rising to relieve himself, had not heard the whickering of horses and seen the first rays of the sun glinting from the Saracen scimitars. His cries of alarm woke the camp—and not a moment too soon. As it was, Richard and his men barely had time to grab their weapons and rush out of their tents. Indeed, many of the Crusaders were half-naked when the Turkish cavalry thundered down on them in its first charge.

Richard's cool head and superb generalship saved the Crusaders from certain destruction. He set his pikemen in the first rank, with the butts of their pikes planted in the ground and the points facing the enemy at a forty-five degree angle so that they would disembowel the Saracen horses. Between each pair of pikemen he stationed one bowman. His knights, with only fifteen horses fit to ride, he held in reserve.

The Moslem cavalry charged in seven waves of a thousand men each, but it was unable to penetrate that bristling hedge of iron points; and when they raced away to re-form and charge again, the Christian bowmen loosed their arrows, killing men and horses in great numbers. "The bravery of the Crusaders was such," wrote Beha-ed-Din, "that we were finally forced to hem them in—at a distance."

Early in the afternoon, when the edge of the Saracen attack had been dulled, Richard led a charge of ten knights against a squadron of Moslems from Turkistan. "He hurled himself at the Turks and clove them to the teeth," wrote Ambroise. "He charged so many times, struck so hard and so often, that he split the skin of his hands. He hit the Turks before, he hit them behind, and his sword carved a passage wherever it fell. If he struck horse or man, it went down."

In the middle of this attack, Richard's horse was killed under him. An unarmed Saracen, leading two beautiful Arabian stallions, trotted up to him through the turmoil. The horses, he told the king, were a gift from el-Adil, "because it is unseemly for so great a monarch to fight on foot." Richard's knights suspected a trick and begged him to refuse the gift.

But the king replied that if Satan himself brought a good horse at such a moment, he would accept it with gratitude.

The fight went on until both Moslems and Christians were staggering with weariness. Toward evening, during a lull in the fighting, Richard rode out between the lines and raised his sword in a gesture of defiance toward Saladin, who was watching from the slope of a hill several hundred yards away. Saladin turned and spoke to one of his bodyguard, a burly youth with a thick black beard. The Turk set his helmet firmly on his head, drew his scimitar, and rode out to meet Richard in individual combat.

As the two men drew abreast of each other, Richard raised his two-handed sword overhead and brought it flashing down with all his strength behind it. The watching Saracens let out a concerted gasp. Richard's blow had cut their champion through from the shoulder to the waist. The Turk's head, shoulder, and sword arm flew off his body. The headless corpse sat motionless in the saddle for an instant, then toppled into the dust.

"When the Turks saw this great blow," wrote Ambroise, "they gave the king so much room that he returned, God be thanked, without hurt. But his mail and tunic were so covered with arrows that he looked like a porcupine."

Richard's victory took the heart out of the Saracens. To many of them he seemed more god than man, for who but a

god could strike such a mighty blow? Saladin was forced to
retire to Jerusalem, where he summoned reinforcements from
Syria and Egypt and set himself, with inexhaustible patience,
to await Richard's next move. The king returned with his
army to Jaffa, still hoping for an opportunity to free the Holy
City.

But the Crusade was over. Little by little during the next
few weeks, more men slipped away to Acre and then took ship
for Europe, until only a skeleton force remained in Jaffa. More
bad news came from England: a number of powerful barons
had joined forces with John and the danger of his taking over
the throne was now acute. Richard, seriously ill once more
with malaria, longed to return to his green and pleasant lands
in Europe. He reopened the peace talks with Saladin's representatives and, after much bargaining, concluded a treaty with
them. By its terms, the Christians would keep all the ports
except Ascalon, which would be dismantled, and the Moslems
would keep Jerusalem and the other inland towns and cities.

Thus, in one of the ironies of history, Richard the Lionhearted, undoubtedly the greatest warrior ever to lead a Crusade, concluded his expedition by treaty and opened a new
era in relations between Christians and Moslems.

On October 9, 1192, after recuperating for several weeks in
Haifa, Richard sailed for Europe. The king lay on the deck

of his galley in an invalid chair, still pale and weak from his bout of fever. He gazed longingly at the retreating shore, at Mount Carmel rising up behind the city. "Oh, Holy Land," he exclaimed, "I commend thee to God. May He of His mercy but grant me such space of life that I may bring thee aid. For it is my hope and my determination, by His good will, to return and restore thee entire to Christendom."

Then he turned his face north, toward his homeland, and resolutely prepared himself for the coming struggle with his brother John and King Philip of France.

TRIUMPH AND DEATH

6

RICHARD was a changed man. He had left on the Crusade full of hope and confidence, certain that "God had smiled upon him and would bless his efforts to restore the Kingdom of Jerusalem to its former glory." He had fought Saracens, illness, his fellow Christians, the elements; he had spent a vast treasure; and now, nearly two-and-a-half years later, he was returning to England with the job less than half done. It should not surprise us, then, that he was bitter and disillusioned, or that he blamed his failure not on himself or Saladin but on Philip Augustus, whom he reviled as a traitor and a coward. Indeed, so strong were his feelings about Philip that for the rest of his life Richard did not dare receive Holy Communion, "because in his heart he bore a mortal hatred for the king of France."

In one important respect, however, Richard had not changed at all: adventure was still the breath of life to him. And so, rather than return home with his English troops by "long sea"—that is, through the Straits of Gibraltar and across the Bay of Biscay—he decided to go sight-seeing in these eastern lands which, he knew, he was unlikely ever to visit again. It was a decision which cost him his liberty and very nearly his life.

The first part of the journey could not have gone better. The weather was perfect, the sea like glass flawed from time to time by a cupful of wind, and Richard did not suffer a moment's sickness. Indeed, as the royal galley made its leisurely way to Cyprus, Rhodes, Crete, and through the maze of islands in the poet Homer's "wine-dark sea," the king recovered his health and spirits. Like any modern tourist, he visited churches and monasteries, and marveled at the vine-grown ruins of pagan temples and palaces.

But Richard lingered a little too long in these treacherous waters, for early in November the first winter gales whipped down from the steppes of Asia and drove the galley to the island of Corfu, off the coast of Albania. Corfu was ruled by the Byzantine emperor, Isaac Angelus, who also claimed Cyprus and who would have been delighted to take Richard prisoner. So the king hastily disguised himself as a Knight Templar and bought passage on a pirate craft that was bound for the head of the Adriatic Sea. From there he planned to make his way overland to the duchy of Saxony, in Germany.

Once in Saxony he would be safe, for the duchy was ruled by his brother-in-law, Henry the Lion, Henry, he knew, would provide him with an escort to the coast of the North Sea, and from there he would sail to England.

But Richard's luck had run out. After a pleasant visit to Ragusa (Dubrovnik), Yugoslavia, a sudden squall drove the pirate vessel onto the rocky shore south of Venice, Italy, and the king found himself in a nest of enemies. Most of northern Italy either belonged to, or was allied with, the Montferrat family, all of whom were convinced that Richard had ordered the murder of their kinsman Conrad. And across the northern border of Italy lay Austria, the territory of Duke Leopold, who had never forgiven the English king for throwing the Austrian flag in the dust after the conquest of Acre.

Richard changed his disguise, calling himself Hugh the Merchant, and set out northward with a few companions and servants. He could not disguise his great height or regal bearing, however, and word soon spread of his presence in the region. He was nearly caught by Duke Mainard of Gorizia, had another narrow escape in the neighboring duchy of Carinthia, and in the middle of December, near exhaustion, he reached a little inn on the outskirts of Vienna.

Had he been content to lie low for a while, Richard might still have managed to slip undetected through Austria and into Saxony. But with typical careless arrogance, he sent his servants into Vienna to buy large quantities of expensive foods and wines. The storekeepers reported these purchases to the authorities, and within hours after the servants had returned to the inn, there was the clatter of hoofs in the cobbled courtyard, the door burst open, and in strode Duke Leopold with a party of armed men.

Instead of feasting on roast goose and sleeping in a warm feather bed, Richard spent a supperless night, shackled to the wall of a freezing dungeon in the Alpine castle of Krems, while Leopold wrote a triumphant letter to his overlord, Emperor Henry VI of Germany (son of Frederick Barbarossa, who had

drowned at the beginning of the Third Crusade), boasting of his valuable capture.

News of Richard's misadventure reached England three months later, in February 1193. It was known only that the king was a prisoner, not where he was being held, so two English abbots were sent to Germany to look for him. Another man, the French troubadour Blondel de Nesle, went to Germany on his own for the same purpose.

Blondel and Richard were friends and had written a number of songs and poems together. The troubadour wandered about southern Germany, strumming his lute and singing verses from ballads that he and the king had composed. One day, the story goes, he sang beneath the castle of Triffels, which was perched on a rocky crag in the mountains of Bavaria, and the king's rich baritone answered from a barred window in an upper story of the fortress. Richard improvised verse after verse, telling Blondel how he had been shipwrecked, how he had been taken prisoner, how Leopold had turned him over to Emperor Henry, and the troubadour responded with verses that told of events in England, Normandy, and Aquitaine.

We have no way of knowing how much truth there is in this charming tale of Blondel and Richard. It is at least possible, however, that the king was discovered in this way, for he was a man to whom strange and romantic things happened.

Finding Richard was one thing, freeing him still another, for Emperor Henry was in no hurry to release his royal captive. Richard made a useful hostage, both for political purposes (the emperor was at war with a group of nobles headed by Henry the Lion) and because Richard was literally worth a king's ransom. It did not bother Henry, a cold and unscrupulous man, that by taking a Crusader prisoner he was automatically excommunicated by the Church. Henry had been excommunicated on previous occasions and had survived the experiences unscathed. His chief fear was that Richard would escape, and so, although he installed the king in comfortable quarters, he kept him surrounded day and night by a guard of burly German soldiers. "To while away the long hours of his captivity," wrote a chronicler, "the king wrestled with his guards, or indulged in bouts of drinking with them, and they grew right fond of their charge."

In the meantime Richard's enemies had not been idle. Philip Augustus launched an attack against Normandy, conquering several towns and fortresses; and Richard's traitorous brother John recruited a force of Welsh mercenaries, took over the English castles of Windsor, Tickhill, Wallingford, and Nottingham, and then crossed the Channel to seek support from the Norman barons. At a conference in Alençon, John told the barons that the king was either already dead or would die in captivity. "If you will receive me as your lord and swear fealty to me," he said, "I will defend you before the King of France. Otherwise I shall let him overrun your lands unhindered."

The barons refused to have any part of this blatant treason, so John went to Paris and became Philip's "man" by swearing homage and fealty to him for all Richard's lands, including England, and by promising to marry Philip's unhappy sister, Alice. Philip in turn swore that he would help John become king, and together they assembled a fleet and prepared to invade England.

But they had reckoned without Queen Eleanor. Although this remarkable woman was past seventy and in ill health, she took vigorous charge of affairs. "By order of Queen Eleanor," wrote Richard of Devizes, "who then ruled England, at Passiontide and Easter and thereafter, nobles and common people, knights and peasants, flew to arms and guarded the seacoast that looks toward Flanders."

In the face of this determined defense, John and Philip were forced to abandon their plans for invasion. Those few mercenaries who dared to cross the Channel were either slaughtered on the beaches or loaded with chains and thrown into dungeons.

Nor was Eleanor content merely to defend England for the "Great One," as she usually called Richard. She put that redoubtable warrior William Marshal in command of an army and had him besiege Windsor Castle, and two other loyal barons closely invested the castles of Tickhill and Wallingford.

Shortly after Easter the abbots returned to England. They had seen Richard and told him of his brother's treachery. The king, they said, had taken the news lightly, saying, "My brother John is not the man to seize any land by force, if anyone meets his attack with even the slightest resistance."

The abbots had also spoken with Emperor Henry, and brought back a stunning demand. The emperor agreed to free King Richard, they said, upon payment of 150,000 marks. "The faces of the chancellor and justiciars blanched," wrote Roger of Hoveden, "for such a ransom had never been heard of before."

One hundred and fifty thousand marks—the equivalent today of about fifteen million dollars—was more than Richard had spent on his entire Crusade!

The people of England had still not recovered from the Saladin Tithe, and now the king's officials set about squeezing the ransom money out of them. Every man in the country, noble or commoner, was taxed one-fourth of his year's income. Churches and monasteries were stripped of their gold crucifixes, silver candlesticks, and other ornaments, despite the violent objections of the bishops and abbots; and those religious orders, such as the Cistercians, whose rule did not allow them to possess gold or silver, contributed their wool clip for the year.

From every corner of the kingdom convoys of mules and sumpter horses laden with treasure made their way to London, where the money was stored in chests in Saint Paul's Cathedral. Not all the treasure arrived safely, for the countryside swarmed with runaway serfs and dispossessed peasants who had turned to banditry. It is from this turbulent period of English history that the story of Robin Hood dates. This colorful figure, who lived in Sherwood Forest with Little John, Friar Tuck, and other members of his band, is supposed to have robbed the rich to help the poor. He was the subject of more than thirty popular ballads as well as of many subsequent novels and plays. Unfortunately, he was a fictional character. Although bandits did indeed rob the rich, it was to help themselves rather than the poor.

In the meantime, having agreed to pay the ransom, Richard was given more freedom of movement. He had falcons and dogs sent from England so that he could hunt, and "scarlet cloth and green cloth and hauberks and capes of doeskin and of lamb's wool and three silver cups." His mother and principal officials came over and celebrated Christmas with him, and Richard prepared for his trip back to England.

At the last moment, however, Emperor Henry hesitated. He had received an offer of 150,000 marks from Philip and John.

They would pay this amount, they said, if the emperor would hold Richard prisoner for another year. By then, they figured, they would have achieved their aims: John would have gained the throne of England, and Philip would have conquered Normandy and Aquitaine.

Fortunately for Richard, neither John nor Philip could raise such a huge sum, and at last, early in February 1194, after having spent more than a year in captivity, the ransom was paid and Richard was freed. As soon as Philip heard the news, he sent John a message which read: "Guard yourself. The devil is loose." In terror of his life, John hid in the cellar of a castle which belonged to his friend, the Archdeacon of Lisieux, in Normandy.

Richard went home like a man without a care in the world, pausing here and there in Germany to see the sights, attending mass in the cathedral of Cologne, and making friends and allies as he made his way to Antwerp, Belgium, where he sailed for England.

After landing at Sandwich, he stopped first in Canterbury to give thanks at the shrine of Saint Thomas, and then went to London. The city had been "crowned" in his honor. Tapestries and gay banners hung from the buildings, and the streets were thronged with people eager to catch a glimpse of their heroic king.

John's rebellion swiftly collapsed. Most of his supporters surrendered and threw themselves on the king's mercy (one of them, the constable of St. Michael's Mount, died of fright when he heard that Richard had landed). Nottingham Castle, however, still refused to yield.

Richard took personal charge of the siege. From London he brought Urric the Engineer and Elias the Carpenter, both highly skilled in siegecraft, to take charge of the technical operations. William Marshal, having subdued Windsor Castle, came with mangonels, small catapults, scaling ladders, battering rams, and thousands of arrows, bolts, chains, and other items. He also brought a supply of sulphur, quicklime, and pitch with which to make a kind of Greek Fire, whose use Richard had learned from the Saracens.

Richard himself arrived before the castle on March 25 "with such a multitude of men and such blowing of trumpets and horns" that the defenders were badly shaken. The king erected his tent so close to the castle that two men-at-arms were shot with arrows and fell dead at his feet. This so enraged Richard that he immediately put on armor and launched an attack. He burned two of the gates, captured some of the outer works, personally shot a knight with his crossbow, and took a number of prisoners—whom he promptly hanged on a gallows which he had erected in full view of the battlements. These measures were enough. Two days later, after being promised that their lives would be spared, the garrison surrendered.

On April 17, in Winchester Cathedral, Richard underwent a second coronation to "cleanse himself of the taint of imprisonment." Three weeks later, on May 12, he set sail from Portsmouth with a fleet of a hundred ships loaded with men and provisions. It remained only to deal with John himself; then he could turn his full fury upon his archenemy, Philip Augustus.

Spies had informed Richard of his brother's hiding place, so the king stopped at Lisieux on his way south to Rouen, the capital of Normandy. "I know you have seen my brother John," he said to the archdeacon. "Do not deny it. Tell him to come to me without fear. He is my brother and should not be afraid. I will not hold his folly against him."

The archdeacon left the room and returned with the trembling John, who threw himself weeping on the ground and begged his brother's forgiveness. Richard had an inexplicable soft spot for his treacherous brother. He raised him to his feet and kissed him. "Think no more of it, John," he said. "You are only a child [John was twenty-seven!] who has had evil counsellors." Then, says the chronicler, "they went off together to eat fresh-caught salmon."

John was fully restored to the king's favor, given lands in

England, Normandy, and Aquitaine, and, provided Berengaria did not give Richard an heir, was promised he would inherit the throne.

Richard's next move was to build the Château Gaillard—Saucy Castle—at Les Andelys, in the lower valley of the Seine River, near Rouen. It incorporated a number of ideas he had brought back from the Holy Land and was a masterpiece of military architecture. Sir Charles Oman, an authority on medieval warfare, said it was "not exactly a typical castle of the last years of the twelfth century, but rather an abnormally superior specimen of its best work." It took a year to build, and when it was finished, Richard looked at it from a nearby hill and exclaimed: "Behold, how fair is this year-old daughter of mine!"

Philip, naturally, was less enthusiastic, for as long as Château Gaillard stood, Normandy could not be taken.

For the last five years of his life, from 1194 to 1199, Richard was constantly at war with his rival. It was a war fought without chivalry, neither side asking nor giving quarter. At a battle in the valley of Andelys, for example, Philip captured three thousand of Richard's Welsh mercenaries. Instead of holding them for ransom, as was customary, he had them all slaughtered. Richard retaliated by putting out the eyes of fifteen French prisoners and sending them back to Philip; and Philip in turn blinded fifteen English knights and returned

them to Richard, the wife of one of the blinded men acting as
their guide.

The bitter see-saw struggle—castles and towns changing
hands, the land devastated, the peasants despoiled, raped, and
murdered—is not worth following in detail. It is a sordid,
ugly story, with none of the glamor or greatness of Richard's
crusade against the Saracens. On two occasions Richard
nearly captured Philip. The first time, in July 1194, Philip
hid in a small country church, while Richard and his men
thundered past in hot pursuit of the French knights. The second time, on September 28, 1198, Richard routed a superior

French force near the town of Gisors, personally unhorsing three knights and capturing many more. Philip, mounted on a splendid stallion named Morelle, led the flight across the river Epte. The bridge broke under the weight of the armored knights and many of them fell into the water and drowned. Philip himself "drank of the river" and was hauled out by his heels.

Throughout this entire period Richard was constantly in need of money to pay his troops. His tax collectors scoured England from end to end, forcing the people to disgorge every last penny in their possession (and causing them to lose at least some of the admiration they felt for their king). It was this insatiable need for money which was indirectly responsible for Richard's death.

In March 1199 a peasant plowing his field near the castle of Châlus, in Aquitaine, uncovered a Roman treasure consisting of gold plates and a number of gold coins. The peasant turned the treasure over to his lord, Viscount Adhemar, who quietly put it into his own coffers. But word of the find got to Richard, who demanded, as overlord of Châlus, that Adhemar turn the treasure over to him. Adhemar refused, and Richard promptly besieged the castle.

Richard regarded the siege as no more than a pleasant diversion, for the garrison numbered only forty men and could not hold out for long. A couple of days after his men had surrounded the castle, Richard was riding along the edge of the moat, amusing himself by exchanging shots with Adhemar's knights on top of the wall. One of the defenders impressed the king by his bravery. The Frenchman stood fully exposed on the battlements, firing his crossbow at the besiegers. To defend himself against their return fire, he carried a frying pan in his left hand. With this curious shield, he deftly turned aside the bolts and arrows that flew at him.

This was just the sort of behavior that Richard admired, and he shouted his approval. The Frenchman saw him, snatched up an arrow and fitted it to his crossbow, and let fly. Richard raised his shield to deflect it. His reflexes had slowed with the years, however, and he was a fraction of a second too late. The arrow penetrated his body at the juncture of his left shoulder and his neck, glanced downward, and embedded itself deeply in his side.

Richard rode back to his tent and tried to pull the arrow. It broke, however, leaving the barbed head in the wound. The camp surgeon, a butcher like most "doctors" of the time, tried to remove the barb. He was unsuccessful, and his dirty hands infected the wound. Gangrene set in, and the king was dying.

In the meantime the garrison of Châlus had surrendered, and the man who had shot Richard, a knight named Bertrand of Gourdon, was brought to the royal tent.

"Why did you kill me?" asked the king.

Bertrand of Gourdon glared at him defiantly. "You killed my father and my two brothers with your own hands," he said, "and would have slain me likewise. Take what vengeance you will, for I will gladly suffer any torments, now that you, who have brought so much evil on the world, are stricken here to death."

Richard turned to his lieutenants and said, "When I am dead you will free this brave knight and give him one hundred shillings from my coffers."

Richard lingered in growing agony until the evening of April 6, 1199. "As the day ended," wrote Roger of Hoveden, "so ended his last day." He named John his heir, although he bequeathed the bulk of his treasure to a favorite nephew, Otto of Germany. To avenge his death, his knights hanged the entire garrison of Châlus, including Viscount Adhemar. It woud be pleasant to record that Bertrand of Gourdon was freed, but in this respect the king's last wishes were disregarded. Bertrand was tortured with burning irons, and then beheaded.

In death, Richard was reconciled with his father, for he was buried at his feet in the Abbey of Fontrevault. Before his great body was enclosed in its casket, the heart was removed, placed in a golden casket, and sent to the cathedral in Rouen. It was rumored to be twice the size of a normal heart.

In the judgment of most historians, Richard was a bad son, a bad husband, a bad king, but a gallant and splendid soldier. This last quality alone, however, was enough to give him a unique place in the history of the Middle Ages.

SELECTED BIBLIOGRAPHY

Appleby, John T. *England Without Richard.* London, 1965.

Brown, R. Allen. *The Normans and the Norman Conquest.* London, 1969.

Gerald of Wales. *Opera.* 8 vols. Rolls Series 21.

Jocelin of Brakelond. *Chronicle.* London, 1949.

Landon, Lionel. *The Itinerary of King Richard I.* London, 1935.

Norgate, Kate. *Richard the Lion Heart.* London, 1924.

Oman, C. W. C. *The Art of War in the Middle Ages.* London, 1885.

Painter, Sidney. *William Marshal.* Baltimore, 1933.

Richard of Devizes. *Chronicle.* London, 1963.

Roger of Hoveden. *Chronica.* London, 1871.

Runciman, Sir Steven. *A History of the Crusades.* Cambridge, 1955.

Stenton, Doris Mary. *English Society in the Early Middle Ages.* London, 1951.

Warren, W. L. *King John.* London, 1961.

Wilkinson, Glennell. *Coeur de Lion.* London, 1933.

INDEX